EUROPEAN BAPTISTS:

a magnificent minority

Edited by Dean R. Kirkwood

CONTENTS

ACKNOWLEDGEMENTS

European Baptists: A Magnificent Minority has required a year in preparation, involving persons in Belgium, Switzerland, Denmark, and the U.S.A. Three of the four European contributors were in the process of changing jobs and locations when their manuscripts were due.

I wish to acknowledge with gratitude the contributions made to this book by Maurice Entwistle who wrote his material after returning to Europe from furlough, to Denton Lotz who completed his manuscript while changing jobs from Europe to Associate Secretary of the Baptist World Alliance in Washington, D.C., to Knud Wumpelman who wrote his material as he took up his new work as General Secretary of the European Baptist Federation, and to C. Ronald Goulding who took up the presidency of the Baptist Theological Seminary, Rüschlikon, Switzerland, after retiring from the Baptist World Alliance.

I would be remiss if I did not acknowledge with deep gratitude the immense amount of work which Dorothy (Mrs. Dean R.) Kirkwood did in technical service in manuscript preparation. Margaret (Mrs. Frank T.) Hoadley has given many hours beyond our normal office time in typing a rough draft and a final draft of this book.

Dean R. Kirkwood
March 1, 1981

Dr. C. Ronald Goulding, President
Baptist Theological Seminary
Rüschlikon, Switzerland

Dr. Knud Wumpelmann, Gen. Sec.
European Baptist Federation
Copenhagen, Denmark

Dr. Denton Lotz, Assoc. Secretary
Baptist World Alliance
Washington, D.C.

Dr. Maurice S. Entwistle
BIM Fraternal Representative
Benelux, France, Great Britain
Bruxelles, Belgium

INTRODUCTION

The purpose of this book precludes it from being simply a history of the Baptist movement in Europe; yet some historical background is essential for understanding what is happening today. This is the first time in the writer's experience that a Baptist mission study has focused on an entire continent--an old continent which has many countries, cultures, and ethnic groups. Only passing mention can be made of events and persons, whereas good historical writing would require several volumes to cover the subject adequately.

In preparing the historical material, I read all of the annual field reports and many of the missionary newsletters for the period 1832-1900. The time slot chosen represents the period of formal development of the Baptist work on the Continent. (Baptist work in Great Britain is not included in this study. Its roots are even earlier.)

The following impressions developed during the reading of the reports from 1832 to 1900:

(1) The Baptist movement in Europe was of God's doing, and it came at a time when his message was being blocked from the masses of people by most of the established churches--Roman Catholic, Orthodox, and State Protestant churches.

7

(2)   God used a few highly intelligent and deeply
       spiritual European Baptist leaders, predomi-
       nantly from Germany, to lay spiritual founda-
       tions for the expansion of the Baptist movement
       throughout Europe and beyond.

(3)   From the beginning of the Baptist movement in
       Europe, the response came predominantly from
       the peasant and lower classes, with some indi-
       vidual exceptions. Yet leaders with signifi-
       cant ability arose out of these underprivileged
       and persecuted people.

(4)   The development of European Baptist work was
       affected by the ethnic, political, economic,
       social, spiritual, and cultural contexts in
       which it was planted. Such contexts influenced
       early Baptist theology and church polity.

(5)   The American Baptist involvement with European
       Baptists evidences God's leading. From the
       beginning in 1832, the American involvement
       was aimed toward strengthening European Baptist
       leadership and churches through limited finan-
       cial assistance and temporary American Baptist
       missionary personnel presence.

(6)   The various British, European, and U.S. Bible
       and tract societies played a significant role
       in extending the Baptist movement through the
       distribution of Bibles and Christian literature
       by means of colporteurs, many of whom were Bap-
       tists.

(7)   It is incredible to realize how so-called
       Christians in the nineteenth century persecuted
       one another in the name of "pure" Christianity,
       totally contradicting the spirit of the Chris-
       tian religion and ignoring the experience of
       the church throughout history.

(8) Baptists have remained a minority religious group within the population of each country irrespective of its culture, national religion, and length of time in which the Baptists have been at work.

The contributors to this book who live and work in Europe today have rightfully questioned the title, European Baptists: A Magnificent Minority. Certainly the title cannot be attributed to the number of Baptists in Europe. Rather it is relevant to the quality of their life which is imbedded in history. The latter chapters of this book tell part of the story of Baptists during the last decade or two. The writers recognize that there are some weaknesses in some Baptist groups in Europe, but they still remain a vital Christian leaven in a secularized society.

Rev. Dean R. Kirkwood, Editor
International Ministries
Valley Forge, Pennsylvania

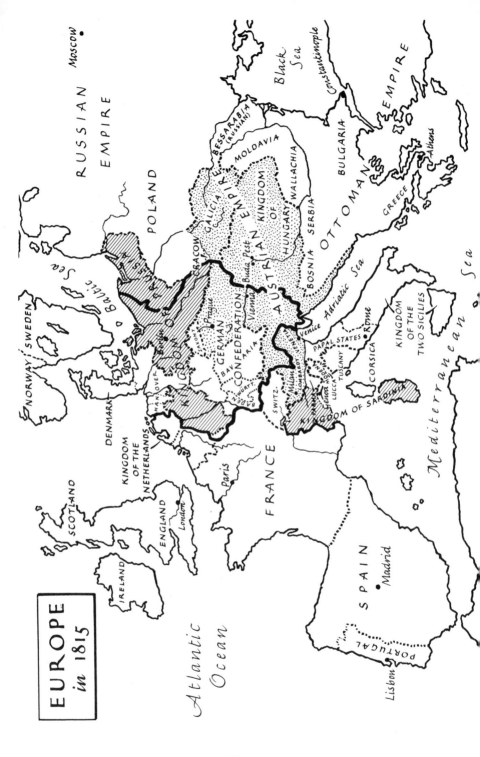

EUROPE in 1815

RUSSIAN EMPIRE

Moscow

OTTOMAN EMPIRE

Constantinople

Black Sea

BESSARABIA (RUSSIAN)

MOLDAVIA

WALLACHIA

BULGARIA

SERBIA

BOSNIA

GREECE

Athens

POLAND

GALICIA

CRACOW

HUNGARY

KINGDOM OF

AUSTRIAN EMPIRE

Buda Pest

Vienna

Prague

GERMAN CONFEDERATION

SAXONY

BAV.

WURT.

BADEN

Venice

Adriatic Sea

Milan

LOMBARDY

PARMA

MODENA

Genoa

LUCCA

TUSCANY

PAPAL STATES

Rome

CORSICA

KINGDOM OF SARDINIA

KINGDOM OF THE TWO SICILIES

Mediterranean Sea

Baltic Sea

NORWAY SWEDEN

DENMARK

HANOVER

KINGDOM OF THE NETHERLANDS

SWITZ.

SARDINIA

FRANCE

Paris

SCOTLAND

IRELAND

ENGLAND

London

Atlantic Ocean

SPAIN

Madrid

PORTUGAL

Lisbon

10

CHAPTER 1

MAGNIFICENT IN THEIR ORIGINS

It is not easy to answer either "what" or "where" were the beginnings of Baptist work in Europe. Baptist historian Robert G. Torbet stated:

The people called Baptists have their roots within what may be called, for want of a more precise term, the Free Church movement, which found variant expression throughout the history of Christianity. Although the term cannot be defined strictly, it is useful to describe the effort of Christians of varying theological beliefs and ecclesiastical backgrounds to restore the New Testament emphasis upon a Spirit-filled community of faith. In essence, the Free Church ideal stressed the necessity of a person-to-person confrontation with God, and so placed only secondary emphasis upon liturgy, formalism, organization, and creedalism in its hardened form.[1]

Europe is the home of three family branches of the Christian religion: Roman Catholicism, Protestantism, and the Orthodox churches. Within each of these traditions there have been a few individuals who were Baptist-like in their feelings and outlook, and some of the strong Baptist leaders of the 1800s came from these backgrounds. Sometimes it was the reading of the Scriptures and/or Christian tracts that moved them to seek a deeper spiritual fellowship. Sometimes an evangelical colporteur or a layman of similar spiritual disposition contacted a seeker at the right moment.

Torbet pointed to three common theories concerning the origin of the Baptists. The "successionist theory" traces Baptist roots back to John the Baptist. Then there is the "Anabaptist spiritual kinship" theory. The third theory is that of "English Separatist" descent. Torbet's opinion is that "the faith and life of Baptists cannot be separated from that of other reform groups of the sixteenth century. Baptists shared with Lutherans, Zwinglians, and Calvinists their protest against the totalitarianism of the papacy and their zeal to recover the spirituality of the church."[2] They are a part of the Free Church movement.

J. H. Rushbrooke, Baptist Commissioner for Europe, 1923, noted in his book The Baptist Movement in the Continent of Europe: "In the year of Waterloo (1815) there were only 4,000 church members. In 1900 this number had increased to some 222,000."[3] We can state that in 1980 there were at least 1,075,881 church members in Europe—probably even more if a true count of Russian Baptists were made. [The Russian statistics often remain identical for two or three years, the latest being 545,000 church members listed for 1977, 1978, 1979, 1980.]

The voice of the Anabaptists in Europe was suppressed during the seventeenth and eighteenth centuries by Roman Catholic and Protestant state governments. But in the nineteenth century a number of forces came into play to open the way for the Baptist witness in Europe. Among these forces were

British and American Baptist mission organizations; the work of the Moravians; the Mennonite influence in Russia; and contacts by Baptist visitors, sailors, and businessmen from Great Britain and America. Perhaps most significant was the tremendous zeal of German Baptists to evangelize Europe.

Biographical Sketches of Some Pioneers

The map of Europe in the early 1800s consisted of a number of empires: the Kingdom of Prussia, the German Confederation, the Austrian Empire, the Russian Empire, the Ottoman Empire, etc. Consequently, it is very difficult to present a few biographical sketches of Baptist pioneers in Europe without becoming involved in the expansion of the Baptist movement and the geopolitical conditions affecting its spread.

The French Baptists who were among the earliest European Baptists confined their endeavors to France's contiguous land areas which we know today as Belgium and Switzerland. The German Baptist movement figuratively exploded throughout much of the rest of Europe, often because of German immigrants living in various countries. A third Baptist force emanated from the Swedish Baptists as they reached into other Scandinavian countries, primarily Norway and Finland.

I am deeply indebted to J. H. Rushbrooke of London whose lifetime coincided with that of the later years of some of the European Baptist pioneers. His extensive knowledge of the work on the Continent eventuated in his being elected Baptist Commissioner for Europe for the Executive Committee of the Baptist World Alliance, July, 1920. His book The Baptist Movement in the Continent of Europe, published in 1923, contains rich biographical information which forms the foundation for most of the following biographical sketches.

13

Henri Pyt, a Swiss in France

In the village of Nomain, in 1810, a farmer found in a corner of his old house a Bible that had long remained hidden and unused. He read it eagerly and lent it to his neighbors, whom he afterwards gathered together. After the battle of Waterloo in 1815, a British soldier of occupation who was a Christian and who spoke French met with the Nomain villagers and explained the Scriptures. They built a small place for worship.

In 1819 around Christmastime, 140 persons gathered to hear the first Baptist visitor to that region, a young man of twenty-three, Henri Pyt, a Swiss evangelist. He stayed with the Nomain villagers a year, endeavoring to establish a new Protestant church.

Pyt and his wife had previously come in touch with a fine Scottish Baptist layman in Geneva. Robert Haldane was one of the founders of the Continental [Mission] Society. Haldane baptized the Pyts. During Henri Pyt's stay with the Nomain villagers, some of the men read an article about William Carey, the British Baptist missionary in India. They also investigated the matter of New Testament teaching on baptism. They asked Pyt to baptize them, but it had to be done secretly in a river near the end of 1820. Ultimately these people organized themselves into two churches—one a small Baptist church; the other a Reformed church.[4]

The events at Nomain marked the formal beginning of Baptist work in France. In turn, this led later to the first two ordained Baptist pastors in France—Joseph Thieffry and Jean-Baptiste Cretin. These two men later became crucial in the establishment of interest in mission work in France by the American Baptist Missionary Union.[5]

14

Casimir Rostan, a Frenchman in the U.S.

The Rev. Howard Malcom, a Baptist pastor from Boston, went to France in 1831 to recover his health. During his travels he heard about some Baptists, and he sought contact with Thieffry and Cretin. He was impressed with the evangelistic opportunities in France, and he communicated with the American Baptist Missionary Union.[6] In the 1832 annual report of the American Baptist Missionary Union is this statement:

> Mr. Malcolm presented the claims of France on the Christian community, and urged the expediency of commencing a mission there. In compliance with the general sentiment of the Board, Rev. Prof. Peck, formerly of Amherst College, and Mr. Rostan, a native of that country [Marseilles], are immediately to engage in an agency for the Board for two years, to investigate on the ground, the possibility and propriety of attempting to diffuse among that oppressed people the blessings of an enlightened Christianity.[7]

The "Mr. Rostan" referred to was an exceedingly brilliant and capable Frenchman whose life was tragically cut short by cholera on July 5, 1834, only thirteen months after his appointment by the American Baptist Missionary Union. Even so, his appointment marked the second overseas field to which Colonial Baptists sent missionaries.

Born into a wealthy merchant's family in 1774, Rostan entered the college of Touran at ten years of age. He had a great love of science [especially botany], travel, archaeology, and languages. At sixteen he began work with his father's trading company, and he spent a year in the Near East where he

became concerned about the condition of the Greek
people--a concern which eventually led to the opening of mission work there by the American Baptist
Missionary Union.

He returned to Marseilles where, according to
the Society of Christian Morals, he began to pursue

his true vocation, which was to devote
himself to the love of humanity, under
every form, and in all the different
social relations which he successively
sustained.... He had scarcely arrived in
Marseilles, in 1799, when he was made
Professor of Botany and Natural History
at the Botanical garden of that city,
and at the same time, he edited a religious and philosophical paper.... He
was soon nominated Archivist of the
city...and elected to the Academy, where
he was, successively, Treasurer, Vice-
President...and for more than ten years
Secretary.[8]

In spite of his success in the academic world,
Rostan "was troubled in the midst of his labors of
charity by the thought that he was too little occupied about his salvation, too little devoted to his
religious convictions."[9] He was one of the founders
of the Society of Christian Morals, "the object of
this society was the application of the principles
of Christianity to the social relations."[10]

In 1825 Rostan was sent to Havana, Cuba, as
the chancellor of the general consulate of France.

He took the opportunity, during his so-
journ in that country, to proclaim religion, make known the gospel, and satisfy
the wants of souls who needed truth.

16

Still attached entirely to the pious duties his conscience imposed upon him, when, in 1827, the office that he filled was discontinued, he hastened to the United States, where...he was received a minister of the gospel; he attached himself to the Society of Missions.[11]

The Society of Christian Morals writer of the Rostan eulogy noted regretfully in his otherwise high praise that "Mr. Rostan, being deeply imbued with the religious belief of one of the sects established in America, kept himself separated from the denominations recognized in France."[12]

Rostan was able to communicate with the elite in French society, and the breadth of his humanitarian concern drew around him persons—secular, agnostic, or religious—who disagreed with his Baptist beliefs but never questioned his sincerity, integrity, and capabilities. He brought visibility to the almost unknown Baptist movement, especially among the intellectuals in France, even though Baptists were often despised and persecuted. Interestingly, upon the death of Rostan, the Rev. Isaac Willmarth, who had been converted years earlier in Paris and who was a recent graduate of Newton Theological Institution, volunteered to take Rostan's place. Willmarth served five years before his health failed. Rev. Erastus Willard succeeded Willmarth, and he became a significant Baptist leader during the next 21 years.

Johann Gerhard Oncken, Germany

It is hardly possible to overestimate the significance of Oncken in relation to the Baptist movement in Europe. His influence has been like a pebble dropped into still water, with the ripples spreading in ever-widening circles. Rushbrooke noted:

The vast majority of the Baptist Church membership of today is found in communities established by Oncken and his fellow-Germans [Köbner, Lange, Lehmann], or by those influenced by them. His name must stand at the head of what may be distinctly named the modern Baptist movement on the continent of Europe.[13]

Oncken was born in Varel, Oldenburg, in 1800, but his father was compelled to flee to England because he had previously been involved in an attempt to overthrow the Napoleonic regime. He died in England. Oncken was confirmed in the Lutheran church at age fourteen, but he had only a nominal interest in the church. At this point in his life he met a Scot merchant who came to Varel on business. The Scot was attracted to the boy and asked permission to take him back to Scotland to teach him a trade as was the custom.

For nine years Oncken remained with the merchant, accompanying him on business trips through England, Scotland, France, and Germany. The Scotsman gave Oncken a Bible and other books, and his first influences away from Germany came from the Presbyterians. Later Oncken transferred to London where he boarded with a devout Independent family, accompanying them to an Independent chapel. He experienced conversion and shortly afterwards visited a Methodist chapel where a sermon on Romans 8 moved him to commit himself to the ministry. He began by distributing tracts, even denying himself food in order to buy more tracts.

The Continental Society, a British mission organization, appointed Oncken in 1823 as a missionary to Germany. He settled in Hambury where he became a member of the English Reformed Church. He preached to eighteen people on January 24, 1824, in a private

house where C. F. Lange was converted and later became a co-worker. Oncken's gift in preaching began
to attract more people until the local state church
clergy forbade the continuance of such meetings.
Oncken then took to preaching at street corners!
He was not yet a Baptist.

The earliest reference to Oncken's Baptist
leanings stems from his 1826 visit to Bremen for
evangelistic services. One of the assisting pastors, Mallet, encouraged Oncken to take theological
studies at his expense. Oncken declined, but he had
already developed doubts about infant baptism--so
much so that he refused to have his first child baptized. He studied New Testament baptism, and then
corresponded with Haldane in Edinburgh who advised
him to baptize himself. He refused, and although he
was invited to come to London for baptism it was not
possible. Oncken waited for a "Philip" to appear.

Rushbrooke's account of Oncken at this period
provides the dramatic continuation of the story.

Oncken, during the years of waiting, had
made the acquaintance of a sea-captain
named Calvin Tubbs, and on returning to
America this man [Tubbs] reported concerning him [Oncken] to the American Baptist
Mission Society of Boston. The substance
of the report was repeated to Professor
Sears, of Hamilton College. Sears came
to Europe in the year 1833, but as Oncken
was about to undertake a journey to
Poland, action was deferred. At last,
on April 22, 1834, he and six others,
one of whom was his wife, were baptized
[by Sears] in the Elbe. On the next day
the American visitor completed a task
whose historic importance he could not
at the time have realized, by formally

19

constituting in Hamburg the first German
Baptist church, with Oncken as its pastor.[14]

Professor Sears reported to the Board in Boston:

> He [Oncken] is a German, a little more
> than thirty years of age, married in Eng-
> land, has two children, is perfectly
> master of the English language, and
> though not a man of liberal education,
> has a very strong, acute mind, has read
> much, is a man of much practical know-
> ledge, and is very winning in his personal
> appearance and manners. From 1823 to
> 1828, he was a missionary of the Conti-
> nental Society, and preached in Hamburg
> and vicinity, with very considerable
> success. Since that time, he has been
> agent of the Edinburgh Bible Society, and
> has had more influence than any other man
> in selecting the publications of the Lower
> Saxony Tract Society.[15]

He was appointed as a missionary of the Board on
September 25, 1835, and served for 38 years, during
which time he established many Baptist churches in
Germany and other countries. He started the first
Sunday school; established a Baptist publication society; started a theological school; organized Baptist associations and the German Baption Union; distributed literally millions of Bibles and tracts;
took extensive evangelistic tours to Holland, Switzerland, Russia, the Balkans, Austria, and Hungary.
He also took trips to Great Britain and America to
raise funds. Rushbrooke described Oncken in these
words:

> Deep in religious earnestness, a sense
> of the grace of God in the Lord Jesus
> Christ akin to that of the Apostle Paul,

a fervent love of the Scriptures, and a
passion for souls, were united with an
almost inexhaustible energy, considerable
powers of organization, eloquent and
persuasive speech, and a courtly grace
of manner that opened the way to men's
hearts.[16]

Frederick O. Nilsson, Sweden

This Swedish Baptist pioneer's name has sometimes been spelled Nilson and Nelson, but the oldest
records list the spelling used in the caption. The
story of Nilsson is intertwined with Gustavus W.
Schroeder and J. G. Oncken.

Schroeder was a young Swedish sailor who had
been converted on one of his trips across the Atlantic. When he landed in New York,

he intended to unite with a Methodist
church, but another sailor invited him
to attend the service with him that day
at the Baptist Bethel [Baptist Mariners'
Church]. During the service Mr. Steward
immersed two converted sailors on their
faith in Christ. This was the first time
that young Schroeder had seen the ordinance, and he was deeply affected, and
said, "This is the way that the Lord
was baptized, and now, it would be un-
grateful for me not to follow him."
This decided the matter; he, too, was
immersed, and soon after sailed for
Gothenberg, Sweden.[17]

Nilsson also had come to the U.S.A. because of
an intolerable family situation caused by his father's
drunkenness. He left home to sail the seas, eventually landing in New York. A Swedish writer, Hj.

Danielson, wrote: "Here God met his lost child, and soon he felt a desire to do something for others who had gone astray."[18] Nilsson became a Methodist missionary of the Seaman's Friend Society, New York, and returned to Sweden in 1839.

In 1845 Schroeder heard about Nilsson. He met him and shared his Baptist faith. Nilsson wrote that through the instrumentality of

> The dear brother Schroeder, the Lord has been pleased to awaken a spirit of inquiry in my mind on the subject of baptism and the ordinances of God's house. The result of the inquiry has been that, after a long and sore conflict with myself, I have at last been obliged to submit to and receive the truth. I was baptized in July, 1847, by the Rev. Mr. Oncken, in Hamburg; and on the 9th of September, this year, my wife and four others were baptized by a Danish brother by the name of Foster [Förster], a missionary by the Baptists in England. Thus the Lord has been pleased to commence a Church on New Testament principles even here in Sweden.[19]

Following this, Nilsson was sent back to the Baptist church in Hamburg for ordination, and he returned as pastor of a small flock near Gothenberg, today known as Veddige--Varberg Baptist Church. On March 5th, 1848, he wrote:

> We now have twenty-eight Baptists! mind, twenty-eight Baptist believers in Sweden. Two years ago, as I and my wife were talking about Baptist principles, we said to one another: "Yes, it is right; if the Bible is true, the Baptist principles

are the only Apostolic, the only true
ones; but no one in Sweden will ever em-
brace them besides ourselves."[20]

The full force of persecution was soon to fall
upon Swedish Baptists because they had fallen away
from the doctrine of the Lutheran state church.

In July, 1851, Nilsson was banished from Sweden.
He took up a pastorate in Copenhagen until May, 1853,
when he, his wife, and twenty-one of his church
members sailed for America, settling in Illinois.
His banishment order was annulled in 1860, and he
returned to Sweden. A Baptist church was established in Gothenberg in 1861, with Nilsson as pastor. Captain Schroeder came back from America and
settled in Gothenberg where he provided a hall for
the church and gave dedicated service. Later he
returned to the U.S. where he lived to age 93.
Nilsson remained as pastor for seven years, and
then returned to America to pastor Swedish churches
for a number of years.

I have only intimated something of the beginning of the Baptist movements in France, Germany,
and Sweden through the use of three brief biographies
of early leaders. Later we shall read something
about other Baptist pioneers in other countries,
many of whom are equally worthy of consideration.
However, Oncken, Nilsson, and Rostan represent early
areas of Baptist work from which the movement spread.
If Oncken had not had as co-workers C. F. Lange,
Julius Köbner, and Gottfried Lehmann, the German
Baptist movement might not have grown and spread as
it did. Nilsson was followed by Andreas [Anders]
Wiberg who shepherded the Swedish Baptists for many
years and saw the movement reach into Norway and
Finland. In France, Rostan's brief work was fol-
lowed by a significant five years of work by Isaac

Willmarth, and by many years of work by Erastus Willard. It should also be noted that often the "missionary assistants" and "native preachers" rendered significant service. The founders of the Baptist movements in France, Germany, and Sweden were persons of strong convictions. They endured persecution, and two of them lived to see the rich harvest coming from their difficult beginnings. But the spiritual growth in each country had been previously cultivated by colporteurs of Bible and tract societies, by British mission agencies, by the Anabaptists and Mennonites, and by a few deeply religious pastors and priests in the state churches.

Notre Dame Cathedral, Paris, France, a symbol of 19th century Roman Catholic opposition to the Baptist movement in France.

CHAPTER 1

1. Robert G. Torbet, A History of the Baptists (Valley Forge: Judson Press, 1978), p. 17.
2. Ibid., p. 22.
3. J. H. Rushbrooke, The Baptist Movement in the Continent of Europe (London: The Kingsgate Press, 1923), p. 5.
4. J. D. Franks, European Baptists Today (Rüschlikon-Zürich: Baublatt AG, 1952), p. 32.
5. Ibid., p. 33.
6. Rushbrooke, op. cit., p. 176.
7. The American Baptist Missionary Magazine (Boston), Vol. 12 (1832), p. 329.
8. Ibid., Vol. 14 (1834), p. 255.
9. Ibid., p. 253f.
10. Ibid., p. 255.
11. Ibid., p. 257.
12. Ibid., p. 258.
13. Rushbrooke, op. cit., p. 17.
14. Ibid., p. 22.
15. The American Baptist Missionary Magazine (Boston), Vol. 15 (1835), p. 230.
16. Rushbrooke, op. cit., p. 26.
17. Thomas Armitage, A History of the Baptists (New York: Bryan, Taylor, & Co., 1887), p. 831.
18. Baptist Work in Denmark, Finland, Norway and Sweden (Stockholm: Ernst Westerbergs Boktryckeri-A.-B., 1947), p. 63.
19. Armitage, op. cit., p. 831.
20. Ibid., p. 831.

A memorial to 20th century Roman Catholic and Protestant missionary martyrs, Gentinnes, Belgium. (Note the shadow of the statue.)

Laotian refugees in Belgium.

CHAPTER 2

MAGNIFICENT UNDER PERSECUTION

Europe in Political Turmoil: 1800-1900

The history of Europe is extensive, complex,
and very long. Through the centuries, invasions by
different ethnic groups swept across Europe leaving
legacies of geographical, cultural, and ethnic
problems which have never been satisfactorily settled. The building of empires through conquest
further complicated relationships among different
ethnic groups, and no country in Europe has escaped
having foreign armies march repeatedly through it.
The immediate period preceding the beginning of
Baptist work on the Continent started shortly after
1815--the end of Napoleon's regime.

The alliances, wars, and suffering caused by
the rise and fall of Napoleon's empire lingered on
through the 1800s. In 1805 we find Great Britain,
Austria, Russia, and Sweden joined against France
and Spain, with the British breaking the power of
the Spanish navy in the Battle of Trafalgar, thus
allowing Britain to rule the seas throughout the
nineteenth century. The struggle for military and
economic supremacy among the nations kept Europe in
a state of constant turmoil. Often royal marriages
of convenience were made in an attempt to build or
retain royal power. Another influence disturbing

the security of various governments was the knowledge of the successful revolt of the American colonies from Great Britain. This created hope for
revolution in several countries of Europe. There
was increased and widespread pressure to get out
from under domestic political tyrants and/or foreign
oppressors and to gain more personal freedom from
the stifling economic system which allowed a few
persons to be very wealthy and the masses to be extremely poor.

Unfortunately in Europe in the 1800s, the
church--Roman Catholic, Orthodox, and Protestant
state--always allied itself with the powerful and
elite segments of society. Often the state and the
church used each other; at other times each appeared
to be an extension of the other. Dissent of any
kind was a threat to their power and privilege, and
if possible such dissent was to be eliminated. It
is into this mixture of political and religious in-
trigue and struggle that Baptists began to appear in
Europe during the early 1800s.

The Kingdom of the Netherlands, 1814-1830, developed following the defeat of Napoleon. In 1814
the Protocol of Eight Articles was agreed to between
the allied powers which defeated Napoleon and the
prince of Orange. "In order to create a bulwark
against France, it was agreed to unite Belgium (the
Austrian Netherlands) and Holland to form the Kingdom of the Netherlands."[1] By 1830 Belgium revolted
and proclaimed its independence. This was resisted
by the Dutch, but British and French pressure changed
the Dutch position by 1833, finalizing the action
in 1839. Belgium was recognized "as an independent
and perpetually neutral state."[2]

The monarchy restoration, 1814-1830, in France
followed Napoleon's defeat. Louis XVIII was permitted by the allies to return to France. A consti-

28

tution of sorts was granted because of the demands of the middle classes. Indemnity and occupation by foreign troops were accomplished by 1818. Under Charles X, 1824-1830, the nobles and the church began to regain power, and repression began first with the press.[3]

Ferdinand VII, 1814-1833, was restored to the throne after the conquest of Spain by Wellington [Great Britain]. "The king had promised to maintain the liberal constitution of 1812, but refused to keep his promise, knowing the absolutist temper of the country and relying on the support of the Church."[4] A fierce persecution of the liberals followed, and dissatisfaction grew in the army. The loss of the American colonies created economic turmoil. Revolutionary movements broke out, and the French army, marching to Madrid, restored order. A more moderate line was then taken by Ferdinand.

In the Treaty of Vienna, 1815, when agreements were being reached following the defeat of Napoleon, Switzerland was reestablished as an independent confederation of 22 cantons. The congress laid down "the principle of perpetual neutrality of Switzerland, restored the old frontiers, with two exceptions, and smoothed over the internal difficulties of the country."[5] A new federal pact restored the old institutions and gave wide autonomy to the 22 cantons. "Racial and religious differences, and differences in political ideals, still existed among the cantons, which made for division and disunion."[6] Between 1830 and 1833 ten cantons liberalized their constitutions--most granting universal suffrage, freedom of the press, and equality before the law.

In Germany, 1815-1848, the country was vastly different from the Germany of later years in terms of the territory it incorporated. The Metternich system [Austrian Foreign Minister] of control devel-

29

oped when German aspirations were stimulated by the Napoleonic wars. The Metternich system maintained rigid censorship, widespread espionage, close supervision of the universities. The Congress of Vienna had called for a Germanic Confederation. "It was composed of 38 sovereign powers; its object was to guarantee external and internal peace of Germany, and the independence of the member states."[7] Metternich viewed the new government diet as representing a loose confederation "to protect German monarchs against their foreign foes (Russia and France) and their domestic enemy (liberalism)."[8]

In the reports of Baptist work in Central Europe, one will read the names of independent states and duchies, such as Hanover, Schleswig, Holstein, Mecklenburg, Prussia, Brandenburg, Saxony, Hesse, Westphalia, Rhineland, Palatinate, Württemberg, Bavaria, Bohemia, Moravia, which today are part of Germany, Austria, Hungary, Russia. Wars and treaties have constantly changed borders and political entities as well as their names. There continues to be a fluctuation between the forces of liberalism and conservatism which has created no small amount of political turmoil in most countries. For instance, Langer stated: "The July Revolution in Paris [1830] not unnaturally had repercussions in Germany, where the revolutionary movement had revived in the hands of the reorganized university movement (1827), in secret clubs, etc."[9] Several German states began to adopt new constitutions in the 1830s, and Prussia escaped the revolution because of its earlier reforms.

The thing to keep in mind is that Germans in particular were to be found in many other countries due to political settlements which changed the borders of the surrounding countries.

Austria, 1815-1848, was made up of numerous

states and peoples, united by common obedience to the house of Hapsburg-Lorraine, and by certain common institutions--the capital (Vienna), the Austrian court, the army, the bureaucracy, foreign service, and the church. These institutions held together the disparate groups of peoples and states until the the feelings of nationalism began to emerge. The Hapsburg-Lorraine territory included the hereditary lands (Austria proper and the Slovenes in the south); Bohemia; the province of Galacia (acquired from Poland; the Kingdom of Italy (including Venetia and Lombardy); and the lands of the crown of St. Stephen (Hungary, Transylvania, Croatia).[10]

Hungary, 1813-1847, started the period under the restrictive reign of Emperor Francis I who ruled for twelve years without summoning the diet which represented semifeudal nobility. Beginning in the 1830s a liberal movement gained strength, having moderate and radical wings. Between the two extremes came Francis Deák who urged a middle course. He sought to assure Hungary its autonomy within the Austrian Empire and to create a modern parliamentary government. "All groups were interested in extending the use of the Magyar language; all favored maintenance of the dominant position of Magyars over other peoples in Hungary."[11] These desires were accomplished between 1836-1844.

Denmark had sided with Napoleon during his war with Great Britain and Sweden. "By the treaties of Vienna (1815) Denmark abandoned Norway [which she had controlled] to Sweden and Pomerania to Prussia."[12] From 1808-1839, King Frederick VI devoted himself to Denmark's reconstruction and financial recovery. Late in his reign representative government with deliberative and advisory powers was established, and nationalism developed.

Sweden was a participant in the War of the

Third Coalition against France (1805) with one result being that Sweden acquired Norway from Denmark,
but it lost Finland to Russia in 1814.   King Charles
XIII, 1809-1818, was obliged to accept a new constitution.   In 1810 a Frenchman, Jean-Baptiste Berna-
dotte, was elected crown prince taking the name of
Charles John.   At this time the Norwegian assembly
declared Norway to be a free and independent kingdom united with Sweden and under one king.[13]

Russia was influenced by Alexander I.   He began
his reign by some liberal reforms--gave amnesty to
political prisoners, abolished torture, liberated
peasant serfs (the first step toward eliminating
this evil).   But then Alexander got involved in a
series of wars: Persian War (1804-1813), resulting
in the annexation of Georgia; War of the Third Coalition (1805-1807), resulting in Russia's defeat.
As a result of the treaty of Tilsit, Alexander and
Napoleon became allies.   This was followed by the
War against Turkey (1806-1812); the War with Sweden
(1808-1809), in which Russia got Finland.   Russian
forts were built in Alaska (1805-1812).   By the
Treaty of Vienna, Russia got much of what we today
call Poland.   Poland revolted in 1830 but was defeated.   "Poland lost its political rights and re-
tained only a small measure of administrative autonomy.   [This marked the] beginning of the policy of
Russification in Poland."[14]

Space and time do not permit speaking of the
Balkan states which have aptly been described as a
"political witches cauldron."   Many of the contro-
versies and antagonisms of the 1800s continue today
--Greece and Turkey, the ethnic divisions in Yugoslavia and Czechoslovakia, the closed societies in
Albania and Bulgaria.   Russia's overpowering influence in this region is both historical and contemporary.   For instance, Russia has had a strong influence on Romania, going back to 1774.

This rather long presentation of just a small
fraction of European history in the early 1800s
should help us to understand better some of the
vicissitudes under which the Baptist movements took
place. The Baptists, like all other citizens of
various duchies, states, and empires, were caught
in political power struggles, changing borders,
restrictions on personal freedom, and often in community hostility because they dared to be different
religiously. Military service, banishment, trade,
and news became means for creating a ferment for
change--a desire for greater control of one's life
and thought.

Baptists' Commitment under Church/State Pressures

Reading the history of the Baptist movements on
the continent of Europe, one must recognize something of the tremendous price the early Baptists had
to pay for their religious convictions. According
to the records there were few, if any, of the early
Baptist leaders in each country who escaped arrest
and/or imprisonment--not once but many times. In a
sense, imprisonment was the government's unintent-
ional "authentication" of the Baptist believers'
depth of conviction and courage. Instead of stamping
out the movement, unjust punishment spread it. When
both the state and the church failed to recognize
earlier history, they repeated it; and to a lesser
degree they keep on repeating it today. P. H. J.
Lerrigo wrote:

> These small bands in Europe, who took
> the name Baptist, often found themselves
> persecuted by government or the state
> church or by both. The stories of im-
> prisonment, exile, and other forms of
> persecution for those who fought for
> religious freedom and other principles
> dear to Baptists constitute one of the

stirring chapters in denominational
history.[15]

The persecution of early European Baptists
took a number of forms--political, economic, social,
physical, psychological, and religious. The reports
which follow have been so selected as to re-create
something of the atmosphere of the individual's commitment. These reports are taken from the records
of the American Baptist Missionary Union [now International Ministries] for the early 1800s. The language is a bit stilted, the punctuation different
from our current usage, but the writers' messages
speak with authenticity, and they need to be read
as they were written. Space prohibits listing more
than a few reports which are representative of the
types of persecution and restrictions placed upon
Baptists in every European country.

Roman Catholic Church/State Opposition: (FRANCE)

By a decree of March 25 [1852], the
President has reenacted articles 291,
292, and 294 of the penal code....
These prohibit any meeting of more
than twenty persons for any purpose,
political, literary or religious, without license by the government, revocable
at any time. No association can evade
the decree by dividing into smaller
ones.... No person can open his house
for even an authorized meeting, without
license. And all persons, parties or
accessories to the forming, or assembly-
ing of unauthorized meetings, are subject to a fine and imprisonment. The
churches are thus placed at the mercy
of the police; the police are moved by
the minister at Paris; the minister is
the mere agent of the President; and

the President is in close league with
the Romish clergy.[16]

The baptized disciples are arrested at
their devotions. Fines and imprisonment
threaten them, and some of them have
been called during the past year, to
suffer for the name of Christ....

With a view to diminish expenses, Dr.
Devan dismissed from his place an assistant at Lyons. With a heart burning to
do good, he travelled out into his
native region, 150 miles west of Lyons,
there to proclaim the gospel.... His
preaching was blessed. Several were
converted, and upwards of twenty were
baptized. He was arrested and sentenced
to imprisonment for three months.... The
evangelist was no sooner in prison than
he began to read the word of God to the
prisoners, and to address them concerning their eternal interests. Four
prisoners became, it is believed, the
Lord's freemen.[17]

Rights of burial, legally acquired and
paid for, have been interfered with at
the instance of the priests, who allege
that Protestants cannot lawfully be
buried in consecrated ground, though the
ground may have been public property set
apart for the common use of the citizens.[18]

Orthodox Church/State Opposition: (GREECE, RUSSIA)

One person in Zante [Greece] has been
added to the little church, and at the
beginning of last year the prospects
seemed more than usually encouraging....

35

But popular violence, excited by the clergy and unrestrained by the government, has compelled the disciples to flee. The enmity of the people began to be excited against them early in the year, by slanderous and denunciatory articles in the newspapers.[19]

The grave political events now in progress, acting on the national and religious susceptibilities of the Greeks and rousing all their ancient ardor against the Ottoman power, naturally casts a shade on the immediate prospects of the mission.[20]

In connection with the disbanding of the female school [in Greece], an effort was made to put an end to religious teaching, as conducted by Mr. Buel in his own house on the Sabbath. On the 19th of November [1847] Mr. Buel was summoned to appear in court, to answer to the charge of having "assumed teachers' duties without the requisite permission, of having collected children of citizens on feast days and Sundays and taught them the sacred Scriptures, and of having supplied them with books on matters contemplated in article 530 of the penal code."[21]

Great awakenings are occurring among the Lettish people [in Russia]. Sixty believers are waiting to be baptized. Meantime, all the converts have been subjected to a judicial examination, and three more were cast into prison, two brethren and a sister. Having papers with them, as is usual in Russia, showing their right to be in the district to which they

belonged, but limiting them to that
circle, they were conducted in chains,
by armed Russians, nearly 150 miles, in
the depth of winter, to the provinces
where they belonged, and there set at
liberty. On the way, they passed the
nights in prisons or in soldiers' bar-
racks, and were obliged to sleep bound.
At midnight they prayed and sang praises,
and the prisoners heard them; their
"songs of lofty cheer," as one of them
remarked, "made the prison walls trem-
ble." They testified of Jesus everywhere, and their journey, often under
a convoy of friends for miles together,
was a triumphal march for Christ's sake
and the gospel's.[22]

Mr. Niemetz, of Memel, writes thus of
the suffering brethren in Russia.
"Things in Russia are growing worse and
worse. In Libau, the two brethren,
fathers of large families, Juraschka
and Pfenert, are still in prison. Persecution rules the day, and the brethren
can no more hold meetings together. The
enemy rages more and more widely, especially among the Lettish people. As soon
as a brother stands up and leads a meeting,
he is apprehended and thrown into prison....

A brother in Southern Russia, who was imprisoned twelve weeks during the year
1862, says--
"Notwithstanding all opposition, the Lord
continues to build up his kingdom among
the German colonists. Nearly every Sabbath we have a baptism, and the number of
our members is, in all, 160. A young Russian wishes to be baptized on profession

of his faith; but here a mountain towers
aloft in our way. It is well known that
every Russian who changes his faith is
to be exiled to Siberia, as well as the
person leading him to such a change.[23]

Protestant State/Church Opposition: (GERMANY, DENMARK, SWEDEN, SWITZERLAND)

Our dear brethren at Othfreesen, in Hanover [Germany], have been most cruelly
treated by the government, at the insti-
gation of the Lutheran minister of that
village. The prohibition against con-
venticles was so severe, that not even
two or three were permitted to meet together for religious purposes. At midnight hours they were visited by gens-
darmes, and pulled out of their beds, to
see if any stranger was concealed there.
Our brethren were thus compelled to meet
in the dead of night, in the woods, for
prayer and mutual exhortation. Bibles
and tracts were taken from them, and
have not been restored.[24]

In Friedland [Germany] Mr. Wruck is in
prison for selling bibles. The judge of
the court where he was condemned, remarked
that personally he would not hold him for
a criminal. He had respect for his religious convictions. But the Prussian
law was before him, and he must keep him
until he should change his convictions or
the law be altered. In his confinement
the prisoners accept his tracts and
bibles, and he preaches to them the
gospel and prays with them.[25]

All the new members of the church have

undergone an examination, and the result was, we were all forbidden, on pain of banishment from the country, to take part in any meeting, or to administer the Lord's supper. It was also intimated to some of us, that we must not for the present leave Copenhagen; unless we meant to expose ourselves to arrest. Not a single member of the church, however, made any promise; but all without exception evinced a circumspection and strict regard to truth, for which we cannot sufficiently thank our Father in heaven, and which gained for us the respect of the magistrate. On Wednesday noon our preacher was again summoned before the court, and required as usual to promise not to extend the church by receiving new members, and not to leave Copenhagen. Declining to enter into any such engagement, he was immediately conveyed to prison; where, however, he has a cheerful, warm room, and other comforts.... My brother is still in confinement, and in all human probability will be banished from the country, but he is quietly resigned to the will of God.[26]

But we still have a severe conflict remaining [in Denmark]. Still the magistrates--slavishly yoked to an obsolete law against Anabaptists, which is pretended to apply to Baptists--continue to imprison, prosecute, condemn, and distrain to the last rag. Thus cows, sheep, and furniture, have been seized and sold from the pastor of the congregation in Western Sealand, because he holds devotional meetings; and, besides, a separate action has been brought against him for administering the Lord's Supper. The sentence will, in temporal respects, <u>completely ruin him</u>.

In Langeland, an action has now for the fifth time been brought against the pastor, and he is sentenced to pay a considerable fine. Several brethren of the different churches are still under prosecution, and <u>must atone for the fines to which they are subjected, by disgraceful imprisonment and living on bread and water</u>.[27]

The authorities have commenced proceedings against the brethren in the provinces and places without the gates of the capital [Denmark]. All who had been baptized since Dec., 1842, are sentenced to fines, and some to imprisonment. The children of the Baptists are taken by the police, by force, to the State church, to be sprinkled, and the parents are obliged to pay the fees and expenses of the same; in default of which their goods are seized upon.[28]

[Frederick O. Nilsson was sentenced to banishment by the court at Gothenberg, Sweden, on April 26, 1850. His sentence read:]

The Royal Court has taken into consideration what concerns this question, and for that Frederick Olius Nilsson has freely confessed to having embraced the positions, that child-baptism, not being commanded in holy Scripture, is only a human institution; that baptism, therefore, ought only to be administered to

40

men arrived at full knowledge of Christian doctrine; and then only with immersion of the whole body in water; and also that the holy communion can be received worthily only by persons of this persuasion; and for that Nilsson, having caused himself to be re-baptized at Hamburg, has in a society there founded, been received as an elder and teacher of the Baptists here in this realm; ...and has caused forty-seven or forty-eight persons to receive his doctrines, and form a separate congregation, to the members whereof, he, in the character of teacher, administers baptism and the holy communion; ...and having been admonished by the chapter of Gothenborg; yet has persisted in disseminating these; his doctrines; ...because, therefore, Nilsson has made himself guilty of the misdemeanor referred to in the code of offences...the Royal Court, in virtue of the said last command, justly condemns Nilsson, for that wherein he has offended, to be banished from the Kingdom.[29]

In some parts of Switzerland members of churches have been thrown into prison for holding meetings and distributing tracts. Still bibles and tracts are liberally spread abroad.[30]

The list of key Baptist leaders who were persecuted in Europe in the 1800s reads today like a list of "Who's Who in Baptist World History." However, persecution and restrictions were not the only arenas in which the Baptists evidenced their magnificent commitment to Christ and the New Testament.

CHAPTER 2

1. William L. Langer, *An Encyclopedia of World History*, Fifth Edition (Boston: Houghton Mifflin Company, 1972), p. 672.
2. *Ibid.*, p. 673.
3. *Ibid.*, p. 678.
4. *Ibid.*, p. 694.
5. *Ibid.*, p. 714.
6. *Ibid.*, p. 714.
7. *Ibid.*, p. 716.
8. *Ibid.*, p. 716.
9. *Ibid.*, p. 716.
10. *Ibid.*, p. 719.
11. *Ibid.*, p. 720.
12. *Ibid.*, p. 746.
13. *Ibid.*, p. 747.
14. *Ibid.*, p. 751.
15. P.H.J. Lerrigo, *All Kindreds and Tongues* (New York: American Baptist Foreign Mission Society and Woman's American Baptist Foreign Mission Society, 1940), p. 254.
16. *The American Baptist Missionary Magazine* (Boston), Vol. 32 (1852), p. 284.
17. *Ibid.*, Vol. 33 (1853), pp. 300–301.
18. *Ibid.*, Vol. 34 (1854), p. 313.
19. *Ibid.*, Vol. 31 (1851), p. 297.
20. *Ibid.*, Vol. 35 (1855), p. 324.
21. *Ibid.*, Vol. 28 (1848), p. 278.
22. *Ibid.*, Vol. 40 (1860), pp. 264–265.
23. *Ibid.*, Vol. 43 (1863), pp. 274–275.
24. *Ibid.*, Vol. 22 (1842), p. 165.
25. *Ibid.*, Vol. 37 (1857), p. 269.
26. *Ibid.*, Vol. 21 (1841), pp. 270–271.
27. *Ibid.*, Vol. 23 (1843), pp. 10–11.
28. *Ibid.*, Vol. 24 (1844), p. 192.
29. *Ibid.*, Vol. 30 (1850), pp. 326–327.
30. *Ibid.*, Vol. 38 (1858), p. 269.

CHAPTER 3

MAGNIFICENT IN EXPANDING THE WORK

It is impossible to trace chronologically the spread of the Baptist movement in Europe. The Spirit of God worked quietly in some hearts, only to be discovered later by those persons called Baptists. There were persons, and occasionally even state church pastors and in one instance a Roman Catholic priest, who were Baptist in their convictions before they ever heard about the Baptists in their countries.

The movement of peoples across the face of Europe due to war, business, employment, and changing national borders often became the means of spreading the Baptist movement, especially among the widely scattered German population. The Europe of 1800 had one face; the Europe of 1815 (after Napoleon's defeat) had another. The Europe of 1871, 1914, and 1980 had some altered borders. Often the new borders did not respect linguistic and cultural heritages of people, and some of these people became minority groups within new political boundaries. Each shift in borders, population, and political conditions has affected the Baptist movement in various countries.

For purposes of indicating the American Baptist Missionary Union's involvement and interest in the

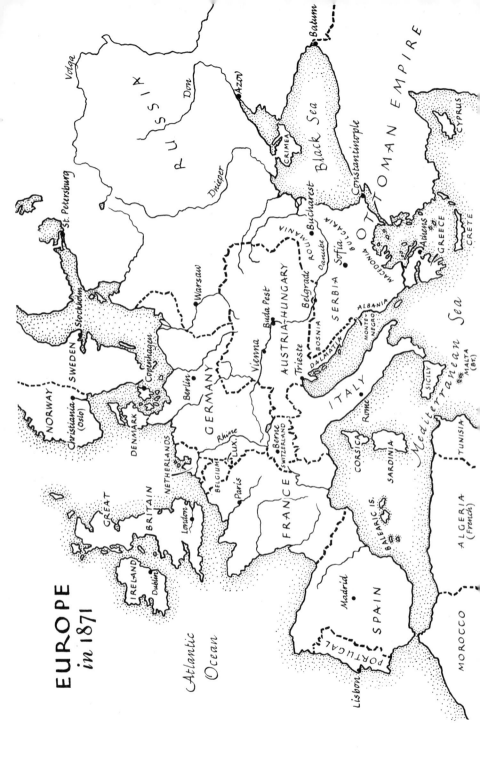

EUROPE in 1871

Baptist work in Europe, we can trace by dates and through personalities the manner in which we moved to assist European Baptists.

The French Baptist Expansion

The French Baptist movement began in a town close to the Belgian border (Nomain), and it was a Swiss Baptist evangelist, Henry Pyt, who guided the Nomain group for a year. These two facts point to two countries where the French Baptist movement advanced. The stronger and earlier French Baptist influence was felt in Belgium. It was considerably later in the nineteenth century that French Baptists reached out to the French-speaking segment of Switzerland, but the earlier Baptist work in Switzerland developed among the German-speaking Swiss. Although French Baptists were directly involved in work in Belgium and Switzerland, it was Casimir Rostan's interest in evangelism in Greece which strongly influenced the American Baptist Missionary Union to undertake work there in 1836.

(FRANCE) We have already referred to the first missionary appointment to France in 1832, Casimir Rostan, whose untimely death cut short a brilliant career. Two other Frenchmen played a significant part in the early development of the Baptist work-- Joseph Thieffry and Jean-Baptiste Cretin.

Two American Baptist missionary families were influential in those early years. Rev. and Mrs. Isaac Willmarth, appointed in 1833, reached France the following year, but Willmarth's health was poor from the beginning. However, during the five years he served, he contributed much through his dedication and fluency in the language. Perhaps the greatest American Baptist impact came through Rev. and Mrs. Erastus Willard who served twenty-one years after appointment in 1835.

At the end of the first twenty-five years of work with French Baptists, the Board's annual report noted the following difficulties:

--The churches were subject to almost incessant persecution.
--They existed in a predominately Roman Catholic population.
--They were a little known new "sect."
--They were maligned in French religious journals with no opportunity for response.
--They feared that American Baptists would abandon the Mission.
--There was an absence of Baptist schools and publishing facilities for cultivating spiritual growth.[1]

At the end of the first fifty years of American Baptist-related work in France, there were only nine Baptist churches, with a total membership of 817 members. The Board's continued unease with the lack of progress in the French Baptist work resulted in a visit to the field in 1867 by the Rev. Howard Osgood and the Foreign Secretary to the European Missions, J. D. Warren. The report by Osgood, commended by Warren, sought to answer the question of the lack of growth in churches in France. Among their observations are these:

(1) First of all, while God has owned and blessed their labor, He has not granted to these churches any Pentecostal seasons, like those experienced in Germany and Sweden....

(2) Then, too, American Baptists have stood in a different relation to the French mission from that to the German or the Swedish.... The French mission has been more foreign to us

than any other to which we contribute.
There is no brother there who can
write English so as to express his
thought correctly....

(3) God has not given to those churches
a leader like Oncken or Wiberg....

(4) Twelve years ago, there were fourteen
workers in our mission in France. At
that time a crisis occurred in the
affairs of the Society, and all but
five were compelled to leave the work
for want of funds....

(5) At present we have no French pastor
who could...satisfactorily supervise
the education of young men.[2]

The Osgood report recommendations were:

(1) We cannot think of any abandonment
of the French mission for any reason
that would not be equally valid
against other missions which we have
no thought of abandoning....

(2) In new movements in the future [we
should] seek for centres of population in which to make new stations....

(3) A moderate sum ought to be expended
yearly in the publication of tracts,
short and weighty....

(4) Particular attention should be paid
to keeping and training the young men
God may give us.[3]

(FRENCH-SPEAKING NEIGHBORS)   By 1861 thought

47

was given to reaching other French-speaking countries. To do this the French Baptist work would have to be divided into two geographical sections or districts. One district would encompass the work north of Paris and reach into Belgium. This was known as the Fédération des Eglises Baptistes du Nord de la France, sometimes called Department of the North. The other district included the work south of Paris and reached into the French-speaking part of Switzerland. It was called Association des Eglises Baptistes Franco-Suisses, sometimes called Department of the South.

A third Baptist work was in Brittany, and this was related to the Welsh Baptists. The founder of the work was the Rev. John Jenkins who left his Welsh pastorate in 1843 to begin work in Brittany.

The Baptist work in France as well as in Belgium and Switzerland has remained faithful but modest. Wars, Roman Catholic and Reformed church resistance and persecution, and the Latin mindset all worked against rapid progress in Baptist expansion.

The German Baptist Expansion

When reading European Baptist history, one must take into account the tremendous impact which the German Baptist movement had far beyond its own borders. Also, one cannot separate the movement from the man, Johann Gerhard Oncken. One writer stated:

> For more than four decades Oncken stood as the undisputed leader of the Hamburg Baptist Church and the German Baptist Union. He was a dynamic person with great spiritual power and talents as a preacher. With these gifts he combined ability as an organizer. He understood the necessity of linking able and dedicated fellow workers to his work, and

everywhere people became very much
attached to him.[4]

Two other persons, Julius Köbner and Wilhelm Lehmann,
completed the early Baptist triumvirate related to
the German Baptist movement. "Alongside Oncken, the
born organizer, stood Köbner, a songful theologian,
whose fluent pen carried on the literary polemic,
and Lehmann, a far-seeing diplomatist, who bridged
over many a difficulty.[5]

Because Köbner and Lehmann played such significant roles in the early German Baptist movement, it
will be helpful to read their brief biographies.
(Oncken's biography appeared in Chapter 1.)

Julius Köbner was born on...the Danish
island of Fünen, and was the son of the
Jewish Rabbi in that place. The conviction took shape within him at an early
age that the Christian religion was better
and more spiritual than the dull mechani-
cal Judaism in which he had been reared.
At the close of his training as an ev-
graver, he entered upon a wandering life
which brought him for a time into contact
with Pastor Geibel in Lubeck. He formally
declared himself a Christian in 1826, but
without any deep inner experience. After
his marriage he settled in Schleswig-
Holstein, where, in addition to following
his trade, he began to write for the
theatre. The Hamburg Senate having offered prizes for the best essays on the
employment of orphan children, Köbner
elaborated the thesis that straw-plaiting
would prove a most effective and useful occupation; and his essay not only secured
the first prize, but led to his wife being
summoned to Hamburg to instruct orphans

49

in the art.

He lived in the neighborhood of the Baptist meeting-house, and speedily heard
that the leader of this small and strange
community was a remarkable orator. He
visited a service in order to listen to
Oncken, and the sermon at once seized upon
him, awakening a consciousness of sin,
and leading to a fundamental change of
heart. On May 17, 1836, he was baptized
by Oncken. His accession represented a
great gain for the cause, for, through
his Hebrew training, Köbner had acquired
an extensive knowledge of the Scriptures,
and he had also enjoyed a thorough and
many-sided education. He was a man of
clear understanding, lively imagination,
considerable poetic gifts, and fascinating
eloquence. By his spiritual songs and
other forms of literary work he rendered
invaluable service for nearly half a
century.[6]

Gottfried Wilhelm Lehmann was born in
Hamburg.... Shortly after his birth his
parents migrated to Berlin, where his
father, an engraver in copper, hoped to
find wider opportunities. The hope was
disappointed, for the storm of war soon
afterwards broke from France upon Europe,
and brought ruin to every form of art.
During this calamitous time the boy
Gottfried was taken in charge by an
uncle who was living in comparative com-
fort in Friesland. Here he came into
association with Mennonites and other
earnest Christians, and through them
was led to God.

On his return to Berlin, young Lehmann
devoted himself to his father's calling,
visited the Academy, and became an en-
thusiastic student of foreign languages,
literature, and music. For the culture
of his devotional life he connected himself with a community of believers which
met regularly for mutual edification.
His keen interest in Bible distribution
led to a correspondence course with Oncken,
and this laid the foundations of their
friendship.

Oncken's baptism occasioned a temporary
estrangement; but Lehmann, as a sincere
seeker after truth, turned to study the
questions raised by his friend's action.
Afterwards he invited Oncken to Berlin,
to explain in a gathering of friends the
New Testament conceptions of baptism and
church order. The exposition convinced
Lehmann, and on May 13, 1837, he, his
wife, and four others, were baptized by
Oncken in the Rummelsburg Lake, outside
Berlin. On the following day the church
in Berlin, of which Lehmann became pastor,
was constituted.

His clear intelligence, firm will, large
power of organization, active enthusiasm,
strict fidelity to conscience, and vast
capacity for work, admirably fitted him
for the position to which he was called.
He developed into a leading preacher and
effective orator [for the next thirty-
five years].[7]

Barnas Sears wrote to the Board on September 21,
1833, urging Oncken's appointment. Sears called attention to the strategic importance of Hamburg.[8] It

51

was the center of commerce for north Germany, close
to Denmark, Hanover, Grand Dutchy of Mecklenberg,
and not far from Prussia. When Oncken was appointed
September 25, 1835, the Baptist church in Hamburg had
thirteen members and two hopeful candidates for baptism in a neighboring town in Denmark. The Board
report for the year 1834-1835 stated:

> During the summer, Mr. Oncken visited a
> considerable number of ships of different
> countries, supplying them with the Word of
> life. The brethren of the church also
> regularly visited "certain districts of
> the city, lending and distributing tracts
> and bibles, accompanied with suitable
> exhortations." Besides the care of the
> church at Hamburg, Mr. Oncken, it is ex-
> pected, will itinerate from time to time
> in different sections of Germany, for the
> purpose of distributing the Word of God,
> and disseminating the doctrines of the
> Cross.[9]

Mr. C. F. Lange whom Oncken had baptized earlier
(1824) was appointed by the Board in 1835 as Oncken's
assistant and as "a colporteur, or bible and tract
distributor." Lange worked with Oncken for a number
of years, his name last appearing in 1849 in the
German Mission roster of leaders. One phase of
Oncken's and his colleagues' work which was very productive was that of tract and Bible distribution (to
be discussed more fully later in this chapter). As
early as 1837, the Board report on Oncken and Lange
stated that:

> 20 brethren of the church are engaged in
> the distribution of tracts and scriptures.
> 100,000 copies of tracts were circulated
> last year, 24,000 of which were on tem-
> perance. The shipping in the harbor are

frequently visited, and tracts given to
various nations.[10]

Tract distribution, itinerating, ship visitation,
correspondence, and preaching became effective ways
by which the German Baptist movement expanded. Even
persecution became a means of spreading the Baptist
movement. Rushbrooke noted:

> They were attacked, arrested, and ex-
> pelled by the police. Oncken supplied
> them with Christian literature, and they
> returned to their homes as missionaries
> to form small Baptist churches. In this
> period (before 1848) twenty-six churches
> arose, and around each a circle of sta-
> tions.... The large centres of population
> became from the beginning the central
> points of Baptist missionary activity,
> thus ensuring for the movement a firm
> basis.[11]

Now let's trace the expansion of the German Baptist movement through the endeavors of Oncken, Lange,
Köbner, and Lehmann. This covers only the earlier
years in each country where their influence was felt.
It should be noted that the first three Baptist
churches established in Germany were in important
centers--Hamburg, Berlin, and Oldenburg. The Berlin
church established in 1837 by Oncken was for many
years under the strong leadership of Lehmann, and
the Berlin church played a significant but secondary
role to Hamburg in the expansion of the German Baptist movement. At the end of the first twenty-five
years (1859), the number of Baptist stations and
outstations associated with the German Baptist movement numbered 756; the number of baptized members
7,908. The data covers Germany, Denmark, Switzerland, and (Alsace) France.

(DENMARK)   It is not surprising that Köbner, originally from Denmark, felt drawn back to his homeland to investigate reports of some evangelical fervor within the state church. As early as 1803, a parish minister, who later became the Bishop of Copenhagen, had an evangelical conversion experience. Similar experiences continued to occur occasionally among peasants and pastors alike.

In 1839 Köbner returned to his Danish homeland, Fünen, an island off the coast. He had a friendly reception and had many opportunities to preach. However, at one meeting he got into a heated debate with Rasmus Ottesen, an opponent of the Baptist position. Köbner was humiliated, and Otteson taunted him by saying he should go to Copenhagen where he could find people "of his own stamp and similar sentiments."[12] He took the taunt to be of Divine guidance, and he went to Copenhagen.

> [Köbner] found there a group of believers gathered about the engraver Mönster, a man who was a convert of the Western Zealand group, but had become convinced, on Biblical grounds, of the impropriety of infant baptism, though as yet he knew nothing of Baptists. Köbner took advantage of the opportunity to clarify their ideas. After his departure he maintained a correspondence with the group, and its members finally decided to leave the State Church. Thereupon Oncken and Köbner travelled to Copenhagen, and in October, 1839, baptized eleven persons to form the first Danish Baptist church, with [Peder Christian] Mönster as its leader. Persecution immediately broke out, and meetings were strictly forbidden by Government.[13]

In 1844 Oncken wrote to the Board: "In Denmark,

the pastor [Mönster] of the church at Copenhagen has undergone a fifth imprisonment; but abides faithful. The church is steadfast; and has lately received seventeen members by baptism."[14] The optimism and aggressive spirit of Oncken which he never lost were revealed in a sentence which accompanied his report on the Copenhagen church. "The Lord is opening a wide field of usefulness for us in that direction, and the question is, now, if our American brethren will go and occupy it."[15] I do not believe he was asking for American missionaries but for monetary support for local workers. Within a short time a second church was constituted at Langeland, then another at Aalborg (Jutland).

(HOLLAND) The Spirit of God is never a respecter of geographical boundaries, and throughout Europe in the 1800s we find evidences of "religious" people having conversions. Holland probably became the second area where Oncken and Köbner saw the Spirit moving. A Dutch Reformed church pastor by the name of J. E. Feisser suffered a series of personal tragedies. At his lowest moment, Feisser had a new personal experience of God's grace and power, which resulted in a dramatic change in his preaching. He contrasted nominal Christianity and true faith. He began to question infant baptism. In December, 1843, the Reformed Church synod dismissed him as a fanatic.

Dr. Feisser had published papers which
drew the attention of German Baptists to
his views, with the result that Oncken
sent his friend, Köbner, to ascertain the
exact position of the writer. Feisser
had hitherto never heard of the Baptists,
but his visitor [Köbner] convinced him
that the only true baptism is the immersion of believers.... He accepted the
practical consequences of this position,

and on May 15, 1845, he and six others
were baptized by Köbner in the open air
at Gasselte-Nijveen. These seven were
formed into a church with Feisser as pastor. Their public action aroused intense
bitterness and even active persecution.[16]

With his typical enthusiasm, Oncken wrote to the
Board: "Br. Köbner's anticipations as to the spread
of the truth in Holland, are raised to the highest
point."[17] A year later Oncken reported that churches
had been organized at Gasselten, Zutphen, and Haren,
and "about thirty members have been baptized. A
foundation has been laid for a church in Amsterdam."[18]

It now becomes more difficult to trace chronologically the spread of the German Baptist movement.
There are two basic reasons. (1) The Hamburg church
attracted persons of many nationalities who returned
to their homelands as unpaid, unprofessional, but
highly effective missionaries. "Some of these brethren have already returned to their native places,
where, according to the grace given them, they testi-
fy for Jesus. Our tracts are of incalculable value
in the hands of these brethren...."[19] (2) Oncken's
co-workers constantly traveled:

The brethren...have recently returned
from their missionary tour through
Meckenburg, Pomerania, Elbing, Dantzic,
Konigsberg, Memel, Lithuania, from thence
to Tilsit, and up the Vistula as far as
Thorn....[20]

Two brethren have been sent out by the
church, at its own charges, to Hungary
and Austria, and "both at Pest [Budapest]
and Vienna converts have been baptized
in the name of the Lord."

...Numerous and extended missionary tours have been made; by Mr. Oncken to Elsass and Switzerland, in which he baptized seventeen converts and organized two new churches; by Mr. Köbner to Bremen and Denmark.... by Mr. Lange repeatedly into Hanover, with numerous baptisms; by Mr. Dorksen in Lithuania; and by Mr. Steinhoff into Hess Cassel, adding nearly forty converts by baptism to the churches in Hesse, though in the midst of violent persecutions.[21]

(SWEDEN)   Sweden felt the influence of the German Baptist movement, even though F. O. Nilsson is considered to be the father of the Swedish Baptist movement [see Chapter 1]. The Moravians had done some work in Sweden. Within a few state churches the pastors and some members began developing an evangelical spirit prior to the 1840s. A Methodist pastor, George Scott from England, began work in Stockholm in 1830, and he was able to work until 1842.

Rushbrooke attributed the beginning of distinctly Baptist work to Schroeder and Nilsson but he noted:

Through contact with Germany and Denmark, two men from Sweden had become Baptists. ... [Nilsson] journeyed to Hamburg and was thus baptized by Oncken on August 1, 1847.

Returning home, Nilsson told his friends of his new experience, and some of them became convinced.... A Copenhagen Baptist minister, Förster by name, was sent for, and he came and baptized five persons.... These five, with Nilsson himself, were organized into the first Baptist church in Sweden, not very far from Gothenberg, on September 21, 1848.[22]

Oncken's report to the Board in 1852 noted that there were four small churches in Sweden, widely separated from one another. Thus, from the German leaders' point of view, the Swedish Baptist work was related to the German Baptists. Oncken wrote in 1863: "The churches in both Denmark and Sweden originated with and have been fostered in their infancy by the German Mission."[23] The Swedish Baptist work was reported along with the German work through 1858. In 1865 the American Baptist Missionary Union took over responsibility for the work from the American Baptist Publication Society, and then separate reports were made from Sweden.

(LITHUANIA)   A German Baptist church was established in Memel, the Kingdom of Prussia, in 1841. This church was on the border of Lithuania and it attracted Lithuanians living on the German side of the border. Rushbrooke stated:

> The Lithuanians are racially and linguistically akin to the Letts [one of the peoples inhabiting Latvia and adjacent Baltic regions].... Several of these were baptized and received into fellowship about the year 1860. After the conversion of a gifted Lithuanian named Albrecht, efforts were made to extend the work to the other side of the frontier. These, however, were largely frustrated by the Roman Catholic clergy, which placed every possible difficulty in the way.... Thus it has come about that the largest group of Lithuanian Baptists is found, not in Lithuania proper, but in Memelland.[24]

In Oncken's report as early as 1844 we read:

In Lithuania our brethren found many believers.... It appears that for many years
there have been considerable awakenings
among the people, through the preaching
of plain countrymen among themselves.[25]

(SWITZERLAND)   Although Oncken was pastor of
the Hamburg church, he frequently took trips to
preach the gospel throughout Germany and in other
countries. In 1847 he traveled in southern Germany
and then went into Switzerland. He baptized a few
individuals at Hochwart. K. Schneiter, writing in
1952 about Baptists in German-speaking Switzerland,
stated:

> In the years of Revolution in Germany,
> 1848-1849, some young Baptists having con-
> tact with Oncken at Hamburg had to flee.
> One of them, Federic Maier [listed by
> some writers as F. Meyer], came to Zurich.
> ... On the 5th of August, 1849, he bap-
> tized eight converts and founded with
> them and several others who were already
> baptized the first Baptist church in
> Switzerland.... The little church had
> soon to go through persecution, but it
> grew steadily.[26]

As is sometimes true, there is a possible conflict in information or in interpretation regarding
the beginning of the work in Switzerland. The careful writer Rushbrooke wrote: "In 1859 two preachers,
F. Meyer and I. Harnisch, were sent from Hamburg to
Switzerland."[27] Schneiter stated that Meier [Meyer]
founded the church in 1849. However, Rushbrook
report confirms the founding date, 1849, for the
establishment of the Zurich Baptist church but without naming the founder. Rushbrooke implies that Oncken
was the founder.

Oncken stated in several letters that there were great opportunities for evangelism in Switzerland:

> An important awakening has existed for some months in different parts of Switzerland. In one village, near Thun, persons from nearly every house have attended preaching in the Baptist congregations. The assemblies consist of about two hundred persons, mostly young men. The ale houses are deserted, and the gospel has wrought a wonderful change.[28]

> Crowded assemblies have met to hear the Word at Appenzell, in Switzerland. Some of the hearers travelled three hours through deep snow.... A missionary, in five weeks spent in Switzerland, visited seven cantons and thirty outstations. When the time arrived for him to leave, he was so earnestly importuned to stay that he yielded.[29]

(AUSTRIA) The great Austrian empire of 1815 was determined by the Congress of Vienna following Napoleon's defeat. In 1867 the Ausgleich (German, meaning adjustment or agreement) provided for a dual sovereignty, the empire of Austria and the kingdom of Hungary. The maps before World War II always use the hyphenated wording--Austria-Hungary. German colonists settled early in both parts of the empire.

After the Great Fire of Hamburg in 1842, many Austrian Catholics came to the city to seek work. Living in Hamburg, many came into contact with the Baptists. "In 1846 there left for Vienna the Austrians, Marschall and Hornung, and these became very active in the city, distributing tracts and holding meetings. They won a few converts."[30] Oncken visited Vienna in October, 1847, and he baptized a

married couple. He visited Vienna twice in 1848
where he was eagerly heard. The opposition to Baptists grew so severe that for the next few years
they could do little beyond encourage each other.

In 1851 the British and Foreign Bible Society
sent E. Millard to Vienna. His house became a meeting place for the persecuted Baptists until he was
forced to leave the country in a few months.

> Eleven years later he returned to Vienna,
> and again brought comfort to the severely
> tried Baptists. The activity of Millard
> eventually led to the formation of a
> permanent church in the Austrian capital.
> This was constituted in his house on
> December 20, 1869, with ten members resi-
> dent in Vienna and ten others in various
> country towns.[31]

The Baptist work in Austria has been difficult, and
its growth has been slow.

(HUNGARY)   It has been observed that the people
of Hungary differ from all their neighbors in their
race, language, and tradition. They are Magyars.
However, they have one thing in common with many
other European countries--they trace their Baptist roots back to Oncken and the German Baptists.
There is an interesting statement in the Board report
of 1860 which refers back to 1845 and to what Joseph
Lehmann describes in his German Baptist history.

> There is a new opening for the gospel at
> Bucharest, in Hungary. Five converted
> Hungarians all left the Catholic church
> together, and were baptized at Hamburg
> in 1845. They have formed a Tract Society
> to which eight families contributed....[32]

Joseph Lehmann's History of the German Baptists contains a passage freely translated by Rushbrooke. It outlines Hungary's Baptist beginnings. Hungarians had gone to Hamburg after the great fire of 1842 to seek employment.

The Hamburg Young Men's and Women's Unions decided to send out worthy young men and to support them in mission work. Accordingly in April, 1846, they despatched [sic] to Hungary the brethren Scharschmidt, Rottmayer, Voyka, and Lorders.... They had received from Oncken some instruction.... Scharschmidt and Rottmayer betook themselves to Budapest, Voyka and Lorders proceeded to Pecs. In all places they endeavored to secure a footing by distribution of tracts and Bibles, and by holding meetings.... Later all united in Budapest. ... They then wrote to Oncken for the service of the mission in Hungary, with G. Kruse as his companion.

Oncken remained in Budapest; Kruse journeyed to Pecs. From that time Oncken held regular meetings in Rottmayer's house, and the membership rose to nine persons.[33]

As early as 1846 a Baptist church of nine members existed in Budapest. Unfortunately, a political revolution soon followed which completely wiped out the Baptist work. In 1865 G. W. Lehmann, pastor of the Berlin Baptist church, came to Budapest and baptized several converts. The Board report for 1866 records:

In Pesth, the capital of Hungary, the few Baptist believers have performed faithfully the part of earnest Christians, and several have been convinced of the truth. Six disciples were baptized near midnight

in the Danube, an hour's distance from
the city, under the friendly light of the
stars, in July last.[34]

Nothing more was heard of the Baptists until 1871
when Johann Novak was sent out from Vienna as a colporteur for Hungary to a place called Nagyszalonta.
Novak found a few members of the Reformed Church who
met regularly to study the Bible, and it was with
this group that he sought to introduce the Baptist
faith.

Three persons--Johann Lajos, Michael Kornya,
and Michael Toth--responded to the teachings of
Novak. Lajos was even willing to sell his house to
secure money for a trip to Vienna to be baptized.
Apparently he was dissuaded. Discussions continued
until 1873 when Novak learned that Heinrich Meyer
had been sent from Germany to take up Baptist mission
work in Hungary. [Actually, Meyer was supported by
the British and Foreign Bible Society, and he was
permitted to engage in Baptist mission work.] Novak
corresponded with Meyer relating the interest of the
Nagyszalonta group. Meyer responded by asking the
group to meet with him in Bekes Gyula on August 21,
1875. At the end of five days of careful examination
of the seekers, he baptize eight persons, including
Lajos and Kornya. Thus the first Hungarian Baptist
church was established. (In December, 1874, Meyer
was responsible for reactivating the German-speaking
Baptist church in Budapest.)

(ROMANIA) Romania illustrates well the difficulty of being a country caught in the crossfire of
two empires and their political manuevering--the
Ottoman Empire and the Austrian Empire. Karl Johann
Scharschmidt, baptized by Oncken in Hamburg in 1845,
was the first known Baptist to enter Romania, coming
from Hungary where he had been influential in starting
Baptist work. Scharschmidt, a carpenter, came to

63

Bucharest in 1856. "He was a zealous Christian, and around him a small circle of believers was formed. In 1856 a German Baptist church was organized."[35] Rushbrooke sketches an outline of several subsequent Baptist developments.

> At the request of this handful of Bap-
> tists, Oncken, in 1863, sent as pastor
> August Liebig, who for four years was
> leader of the church and conducted the
> earliest celebrations of baptism. The
> locksmith, Friedrich Weigel, who settled
> in Bukarest in 1864, proved in later
> years to be a tower of strength. Oncken
> himself visited the church in 1869.

> Meanwhile Baptist colonists from Russia
> were settling in the delta of the Danube--
> then Turkish territory, and among these
> immigrants and German colonists of the
> same district a number of Baptist churches
> arose.[36]

Once again we must mention the contribution of the British and Foreign Bible Society to Baptist work. It was through the cooperation of Edward Millard, director of the Bible depot in Vienna, that a manager-pastor, Daniel Schwegler, was sent to Bucharest in 1878.

As far as we know, the first Hungarian-speaking Baptist church was formed in Salonta More in 1871. Much of what we now know as the Romanian Baptist movement occurred after 1900. A Romanian named Constantin Adorian, a business man, attended the 1908 European Baptist Congress. He decided to study for three years at the Hamburg Seminary. Later he returned to Romania to found in 1911 or 1912 the first Romanian Baptist church.

The year 1919 brought a great transfer
of territory to Rumania, and the newly
acquired lands included so many Baptist
churches that except in Russia, Sweden,
and Germany the membership is not exceeded
by any country of continental Europe.[37]

(POLAND)   Poland's territorial and linguistic/
cultural problems have been historically similar to
those of Romania. Portions of the historic Poland
have been ruled or dominated by Germany, Austria,
and Russia. Thus mission work has required a half a
dozen languages and different approaches. Rushbrooke
stated: "It was difficult...to win Polish converts,
especially in view of the widespread idea that national loyalty and Roman Catholicism belonged together and that to become a Protestant was to cease
to be a good Pole."[38]   Furthermore, the Baptist message was carried initially by citizens from countries
which ruled Poland.

There were several separate Baptist beginnings
in Poland, the earliest coming through the German
Baptist movement. The Board report covering the year
1857 stated:

An awakening has occurred on the Polish
frontiers. A German brother having business in that region distributed tracts,
one of which, falling into the hands of
an aged lady, led to the holding of an
evening meeting, at which sixty souls
were present. The tidings quickly spread
to the neighboring village, and much in-
quiry for the truth and an earnest desire
to have regular meetings is the result.[39]

It is interesting to note that the earliest Baptist movement in Poland occurred among German colonists living in a section of Poland which was under

65

Russian rule.

> On Sunday, November 28, 1858, at Adamow,
> nine persons, converted under the influ-
> ence of German Baptists, were baptized.
> Among these was a young teacher, Gottfried
> Alf, who became a pioneer in this region
> of a vigorous evangelistic work.... It was
> in vain that the clergy of the State
> churches and Russian officials endeavored
> to strangle the movement by stern pro-
> hibitions, arrests and imprisonments....
>
> Alf showed his remarkable qualities as
> a leader. His wisdom was mated with a
> courage that, during the forty years fol-
> lowing his conversion, never failed. He
> was ten times imprisoned; but after a few
> years the severity of persecution died
> down in accordance with the general ten-
> dency of the Russian administration to
> tolerate "sectarian" movements so long
> as they did not directly affect Russian
> Orthodox communities.[40]

Adamow is the place where the first Baptist church
in Poland was founded, and it was from here that the
Baptist work later spread to mid-Russia.

A second significant Baptist center developed
at Kicin [sometimes spelled Kiciny], beginning in
1860 when Alf preached in a Mennonite meeting.
Their leader, Ewert, and many others were converted.
Alf than transferred his residence to Kicin where
he carried on mission work made possible by the support of a Baptist church in Scotland. By 1900 there
were 4,162 Baptists in Poland of whom there were only
200 Slavs, and these were mainly Bohemian settlers.

In Alf's letters to the Board there is evidence

66

that some Poles were converted under his ministry: "Fifty-three Poles have been baptized during the year."[41] In 1861 he wrote that the future looked very favorable for sowing the seed of the gospel. According to Rushbrooke, the few separate Polish churches have existed only since 1921, which is beyond the historical time period, 1832-1900, this section of Baptist history covers.

(RUSSIA)   Baptist work in Russia originated in three different areas and under different influences. Two movements came from the efforts of the German Baptists. However, let us look at the third movement first--the English connection. Associated with it is the Baptist movement among the Slavs and the development of the All-Russian Union of Evangelical Churches. The beginnings were beautifully described by Rushbrook.

> A simple and moving story stands at the
> opening of the record. In the year 1865
> a twelve-year-old boy, belonging to an
> aristocratic family, was lying fatally
> ill in Petrograd. He had become a Chris-
> tian under the influence of a tutor, but
> had tried in vain to win his very worldly
> mother. The boy's last testimony and ap-
> peal, however, left a deep impression,
> and she became a seeker after Christ.
> This lady (Mrs. E. S. Tchertkowa), having
> found no preaching in Petrograd that
> answered her need, undertook a journey
> abroad, in the course of which she heard
> Lord Radstock preach. She invited him to
> visit the Russian capital, and this he
> did in 1870, and on two occasions in later
> years, preaching in the houses of leading
> families with extraordinary effect. Count
> Bobrinsky, at one time a Minister of State,
> became a convert, and others included Count

M. M. Korff and Colonel Pashkoff. These
began to tell the Gospel story to their
workpeople and the peasants on their es-
tates, to print and distribute tracts,
and to organize Christian philanthropic
efforts. Slowly at Petrograd and elsewhere churches came into existence.[42]

Colonel Pashkoff and his fellow workers learned
about the evangelical movement in southern Russia
sometimes called "Stundist" or "Baptist." In 1883
leaders of the Stundist/Baptist movement were invited
to Petrograd to confer about the possibility of forming a Union. The Orthodox clergy and the government
got wind of the proposal and prevented the meeting,
exiling Pashkoff and Korff from Russia. Prokhanoff,
converted to the Baptist faith in the Caucasus, came
to the Technological Institute in Petrograd in 1888.
He became very active among the Baptists and "set
before himself as life-purpose the development of
the evangelical movement...and the securing as much
influence as possible with the leaders of the Orthodox Church, in order to promote a reformation in
that body."[43] Prokhanoff earned his living as an
engineer and assistant professor, but he gave himself
to evangelical work, publishing a hymnbook (500 songs
of his own composition) and periodicals. It was not
until 1909 that the government permitted the holding
of the first All-Russian Evangelical Christian Conference.

The German Baptist work in Russia had its roots
among German settlers who were affected by a revival
movement during the 1830s and 1840s in the south of
Russia. Pastor Wuest, a Mennonite, and Pastor Bonne-
kemper who worked among the Lutheran and Reformed
communities, led a number of persons to the New
Testament Baptist position on baptism and personal
faith. It was in 1864 that the first baptism by immersion was performed in south Russia. Soon German-

speaking churches were formed in Alt-Dantzig, Johamistal, Neuberg, Odessa, and elsewhere. Among the pioneer German evangelists were August Liebig, K. Fullbrandt, and Klundt.

German Baptist work spread as new German colonizers moved into different parts of Russia. "The colonisation of Siberia was largely accomplished by German Baptists, among whom were not a few of the newly-won Baptists."[44] Eventually a Union of German Baptists in Russia was formed, comprising six Associations scattered across the land.

Finally, we must consider Russia proper—particularly in Kherson and Transcaucasia. The German Baptist influence was felt, and the Russian converts called themselves Baptists. The first Russian advocate of Baptist principles was a peasant, Ivan Rjaboschapka, in the village of Lubomirka, Kherson. The peasant had talked with a Baptist German blacksmith, Martin Hubeer. Even though Rjaboschapka desired baptism, he could not get it because the Germans were afraid of retaliation from the Russian Government. Another peasant found a way to succeed and to help Rjaboschapka.

> On June 11, 1869, a converted Russian peasant named Zimbal had contrived to introduce himself among a group of thirty persons awaiting baptism by a visiting pastor at the German Baptist church of Alt-Dantzig. Since none of the resident Baptists, to whom he was well known, called attention to his presence, he was immersed with the others. This man [Zimbal] shortly afterwards baptized Rjaboschapka, and he in turn Ratuschny, who became his fellow-pioneer in the Khersonese movement.[45]

The Transcaucasia Baptist beginnings also involved a German Baptist and a Russian seeker. Martin Kalweit, a humble artisan living in Lithuania, had been reared a Lutheran, but he was dissatisfied in his religious life. Having heard about the Baptists in East Prussia, he crossed the border to Memel to learn more. He was baptized in 1858, and in 1862 he migrated to Tiflis. In time a Russian merchant, Nikita Voronia, came into contact with Kalweit. He became convinced of the Baptist way, and was baptized by Kalweit in 1867. By 1870 there was a small Baptist church with seven or eight members.

Early in 1871 a sixteen-year-old boy, Vasili Pavloff, who had been reared a Molokan,* was baptized. The boy began to preach with power, and in 1875 he was sent to Hamburg for brief pastor training. Oncken ordained him in 1876. As he returned to Voronia, he met Ratuschny who was linked with the Baptist work in Kherson. This meeting resulted in the formation of a preliminary connection between the Baptist work in Transcaucasia and Kherson.

One final word on Russia and Oncken. At age 69, Oncken included Russia on his evangelistic tour, writing afterward: "My mission to Russia has been attended with happy results. Three churches have been formed in the south of Russia, numbering 300 immersed believers."[46] Four years earlier Oncken and a colleague made a trip to Russia with the intent to plead for religious liberty for the Baptist brethren, but they were denied access to government officials. Even though their main purpose was frustrated, they baptized seven converts!

(BULGARIA) Baptist work in Bulgaria has part of its roots in the German Baptist movement. The

---

*The Molokans rejected oaths, military service, and the ordinances of baptism and the Lord's Supper.

Board report for 1865 noted: "In the mountains of
Bulgaria twenty-two converts have recently been baptized by pioneer missionaries lately sent forth from
Hamburg."[47] Rushbrooke noted that although there had
been some work done in the country by German and
Russian Baptists (including Vasili Pavloff) in the
1860s, there was no systematic missionary enterprise.
"Small isolated groups of converts existed and la-
boured, largely in ignorance of one another and the
outside world. Terrible wars again and again reduced
their membership."[48]

The founder of the first Baptist church in Bulgaria was Kargel, a German evangelist from St. Peters-
burg, Russia. He was supported by the Russian noble-
man, Colonel Pashkoff.

Kargel came to Bulgaria in 1880, and
found four German Baptists in Rustchuk
and Lom-Palanka, and a group of Bulgarians in Kazanlik...who by the study
of the New Testament, had come to
understand the significance of believers' baptism.[49]

Kargel went to Kazanlik where he baptized eight converts and organized the first Baptist church in the
country. Another Baptist church was also organized
in 1880 in Rustchuk, with Kargel as its pastor.

The British and Foreign Bible Society sent
August Klundt as a colporteur to Üskub, Macedonia,
but persecution drove him to Bulgaria where he worked
in Lom-Palanka, founding several churches. One of
his early converts was a gypsy, Peter Puntscheff, who
established a church among the gypsies in Golinzi.

Rudén and Lahrson pointed out that another
"source of Baptist activity was the Bulgarians who
had come into contact with Baptists outside, return-

ing to their home to preach Baptist principles."[50]
Generally, these outside contacts came after 1900.

(CZECHOSLOVAKIA)   The nation we know today as
Czechoslovakia did not exist until 1918, but some
of its component ethnic groups go back to the fifth
century. The Czechs founded the Kingdom of Bohemia,
but for 300 years they were a part of the Austrian
Empire. Today the country has significant groups of
Czechs and Slovaks, and minority groups of Germans,
Hungarians, Poles, and Ukrainians. Not surprisingly,
the German-speaking population became the first contact for the Baptist message.

A. Meeris, a colporteur of the British and Foreign Bible Society worked in Bohemia, and on April 14,
1877, he baptized five persons at Brandys. Thereafter he was not permitted to continue his work, so
he moved to Slovakia then under Hungarian rule. As
early as the 1860s another German Baptist, A. Knappe,
had baptized people in Bohemia, but he did not organize them into a church.

A key leader in Czechoslovakia was Henry Novotny,
a friend of Meeris. Novotny had trained for the Congregational ministry, but later he accepted Baptist
views. He was baptized in 1885 at Lodz, Poland.   "On
his return to Bohemia the first Baptist church was
founded at Hledsebe, near Prague, on March 25, 1885.
It consisted of sixteen members, who elected Novotny
as their pastor."[51] He is the person who laid the
permanent foundations of the Baptist work in Bohemia,
now part of Czechoslovakia.

(YUGOSLAVIA)   This is another 1918 politically-
created country consisting of former republics under
the Austria-Hungary monarch. The republics include
Serbia, Croatia, Slovania, Bosnia, Herzegovina,
Macedonia, and Montenegro.

72

The earliest Baptist activity appeared
among the Germans in 1875, when Adolf
Hempt was converted in Novisad [today
Novi Sad]. He became, like many other
Baptists in south-eastern Europe, a colporteur of the British and Foreign Bible
Society, travelling in Bosnia, Herzegovina
and Serbia. Baptist advance was furthered
by the missionary zeal of Heinrich Meyer,
of Budapest, who extended his evangelistic journeys over all parts of the former
Hungary.[52]

In 1863 Oncken sent one of his effective workers,
August Liebig, to South Russia. Enroute he made a
journey through Serbia and Western Bosnia, baptizing
a few converts along the way. Other converts came
when soldiers and workers from the region were sent
abroad during the not infrequent wars.

Nicola Zrincak, of Zagreb, was baptized by Heinrich Meyer in 1883. This lay preacher worked for
forty years in his native Croatia.

(BALTIC REPUBLICS) Three Baltic republics--
Estonia, Latvia, and Lithuania--have enjoyed only a
short independence period, occurring between World
War I and II. Today they are incorporated into the
U.S.S.R. Always they have been strongly influenced
and often dominated by their larger neighbors--
Poland, Germany, Russia, Finland, and even Denmark
and Sweden. The German and Russian influence has
been strong during the last two centuries in both
culture and religion.

The German Baptist movement came to Lithuania
rather early through the Baptist church which Oncken
established in Memel, East Prussia, in 1841. This
church won some Lithuanians who had crossed the border
of Prussia. Several were received into the Memel

church in 1860. A man whose name was Albrecht was the first known convert. Most of the Baptist work has remained among the Lettish people. Mission work was begun in Lithuania in 1879, coming from East Prussia. An independent Lithuanian Baptist organization was established in 1889. Otto Lenz was a significant Baptist pastor during this period.

Estonia, the farthest north republic, has an affinity linguistically and racially with Finland. In 1877 something of a religious awakening occurred, beginning first with the Swedish residents in Lithuania. Persons began to take theological and practical positions which differed from the established church. Great persecution broke out. Rushbrooke noted:

> The preparatory period of the regularly organized Baptist work may be regarded as including the years 1877 to 1884. The believers knew nothing of Baptists, but the reading of the scriptures had led them to reject infant baptism.... They sought instruction from a German Baptist pastor in Petrograd [Russia], who on February 11, 1884, first performed the New Testament rite by immersion, at Hapsal, [of] nine persons.[53]

The next day other persons were baptized in ice water, the air temperature being 13 degrees below zero! Soon afterward riots erupted against the Baptists.

Latvia, the middle republic, had many Lettish people. As early as the 1840s there were groups of people who gathered outside of the established church for prayer and Bible reading. During the Crimean War, 1853-1856, unemployment forced some Latvians to go to Memel. "Among the emigrants was a young ship's carpenter named Jakobsohn, who came into contact with the Baptist church in Memel and was baptized there

in 1855."[54] He was the first Lettish Baptist.
Others joined the Memel church until there were
fourteen Lettish members in 1859. Other persons
crossed the border under threats and persecution in
order to be baptized at Memel. Two such persons
were E. Gaertner and E. Eglit who labored valiantly
to establish Baptist churches in Latvia. The first
baptism on Latvian soil occurred in early September,
1861, when A. Gaertner administered the ordinance
to seventy-two persons. Persecutions continued,
but the Czar's government finally allowed the Baptists freedom in 1879. Until 1875 Latvian Baptists
looked upon the Memel church as the mother church.
After 1875 Lettish conferences were held annually.

The German Baptist expansion during the 1800s
was truly remarkable. Although our immediate interest is in Europe, we must recognize that German Baptist churches sprang up in Turkey, Africa, Australia,
and particularly the U.S.A. Due credit must be given
to the British and Foreign Mission Society and to
the National Bible Society of Scotland which supported many German Baptist colporteurs. We should
not forget that Baptists in England, Scotland, and
Wales provided financial support to many German
Baptist endeavors. And over all looms the towering
figure of J. G. Oncken whose guiding hand, unlimited
energy, wise strategy, and burning evangelistic passion dominated the German Baptist movement for
nearly 50 years.

The Swedish Baptist Expansion

The third center for the expansion of Baptist
work in Europe in the 1800s was Sweden, primarily
reaching its immediate neighbors--Norway and Finland.
Inadvertently and unintentionally the Swedish Baptists also enabled American Baptists to enter mission
work in the Philippines in 1900. The American Baptist Missionary Union appointed Eric Lund, the

Swedish Baptist missionary who was serving in Spain. In Chapter 1 we presented a brief biography of F. O. Nilsson who is considered to be the founder of the Swedish Baptist movement. Now, however, we will present other significant Baptist personalities and events relating to the Swedish Baptist expansion.

(SWEDEN)   Prior to the Baptist beginnings in Sweden, a Methodist pastor from England, George Scott, began mission work in Stockholm in 1830. There was already some ferment within the Lutheran church due to the Pietist movement which touched much of Europe. However, there was a general lack of spiritual vitality in many state churches. Without breaking away from the state church, a number of Lutherans held private views and reservations regarding certain church practices, particularly infant baptism. Some met in private homes for spiritual worship. They were punished when discovered. Scott's preaching produced believers on the one hand and fierce government/clergy opposition on the other. He was finally forced to leave Stockholm in 1842.

The first Baptist church in Sweden was established near Gothenberg in 1848. F. O. Nilsson had been baptized by Oncken in July of 1847 at Hamburg. A Copenhagen Baptist pastor, Förster, came to Sweden at Nilsson's request to baptize Nilsson's wife and four other persons on September 21, 1848, and to form the church. In 1851 Nilsson was banned from Sweden, but already the Baptist work had spread beyond Stockholm. Oncken's report on the Swedish work for 1852 stated:

> In Sweden, the prospects of the four
> little churches, at Gottenburg, Berghinn,
> Waro, and Unsala, are very dark, from the
> iron pressure of persecution. For refus-
> ing to have their infants christened, they
> have been fined till they are reduced to

great want. The church at Hamburg has rendered the brethren some aid, but it is feared that no choice will be left them between emigration and entire beggary.[55]

Indeed it is true that God sometimes works in mysterious ways. Nilsson was in exile. The fledgling Baptist movement was under persecution. But a young man, Andreas [later called Anders] Wiberg had previously come under the influence of Methodist George Scott sometime between 1830 and 1842 while he was a student at the University of Upsala. Wiberg became a state church clergyman for six years, but he was drawn to the Pietists. He was criticized and threatened by state church authorities until he resigned his pastorate and joined the Pietists in Stockholm. But Wiberg still defended infant baptism, and he prepared to write a book against the "Anabaptist errors."

Somehow contact was made between Wiberg and the Hamburg Baptists. Wiberg was invited to visit Hamburg where he defended the Lutheran position on baptism in a discussion with Oncken and Köbner. As he departed, Köbner gave Wiberg a pamphlet on baptism. He read it, and he became convinced that the Baptists were right. He went ahead and wrote his book on baptism, but it now became a defense of the Baptist position! The book had a significant influence in Sweden and beyond.

Wiberg's health began to fail, and he started a trip to America, stopping off first in Copenhagen to talk with Swedish Baptist Nilsson who baptized him July 23, 1852. During his three years in the U.S.A., Wiberg engaged in mission work at Mariners' Church in New York. In Sweden the Baptists desperately needed leadership, so they sent two of their number, D. Forsell and P. F. Heijdenberg [Heijdenberg is also spelled Heydenberg in the German reports] to

Hamburg. Both men were furriers by trade.

They were sent to Hamburg at the instance
of hundreds of believers who had left the
national church and who had formed themselves into churches in various parts of
Sweden, and have been for several years
anxiously waiting for baptism. In the
name of these brethren, it was solicited
that one of these persons, Mr. Heydenberg,
should be empowered to administer the
sacraments. After the most thorough
examination and serious deliberation, the
brethren at Hamburg fulfilled the request.
After his return to Sweden, Mr. Heydenberg
prosecuted his labors with much diligence.
At Elfdalen, sixty-six believers were baptized, and a church formed.[56]

A year later, 1855, Wiberg would reenter the
Baptist work in Sweden under the auspices of the
American Baptist Publication Society "to provide for
the establishment of a system of Colportage in
Sweden."[57] He was commissioned a missionary on
July 1, 1855, and left for Sweden in September. Six
years after his return we read in Board minutes:

Rev. A. Wiberg is performing a great and
varied work. He superintends the entire
colporteur force in Sweden, conducts all
the correspondence, is the pastor of the
Church in Stockholm, edits and publishes
a semi-monthly paper, also many tracts,
lectures on Theology three times each week
during the winter in Colporteur school at
Stockholm, and is engaged in preparing a
commentary on the New Testament, after the
style of Henry.[58]

There have been a number of other Baptists who

contributed greatly to the work in Sweden, but Wiberg's contribution looms large during the early years and the expansion of the work. In the ten-year period between 1855 and 1865, the Baptist churches' membership increased from 300 to 6,411. It continued to grow in the 1800s making it one of the larger Baptist groups.

In March, 1866, the Swedish Mission's relationship with American Baptists was changed from the American Baptist Publication Society to the American Baptist Missionary Union. The Board minutes recorded:

> Rev. Andreas Wiberg and Rev. Knut Oscar Broady, both natives of Sweden, were appointed missionaries of the Union, to labor in their native country. At the same time the Executive Committee assumed the support of twelve other persons, all but two or three of whom had before been laboring under the patronage of the Publication Society.... Mr. John Alexis Edgren, also a Swede by birth, appeared before them, and received an appointment to labor in the same field....[59]

Throughout the remainder of the 1800s there were periodic times of revival and periodic economic recessions and subsequent emigrations. The Baptist work expanded beyond the borders of Sweden. Baptist organizations and institutions were established within the country. The Swedish Baptists developed several strong Missionary Unions. For instance, it is recorded in the Board report for 1881 that

> The Stockholm Missionary Union has supported 20 evangelists in Sweden and Norway, entirely or in part, at an expenditure of 7,462 crowns (about $2,800).... The work has extended to all Sweden,

except two of the western counties; also to some parts of Finland and Norway.[60]

(NORWAY) The groundwork for opening Baptist work in Norway was unintentionally laid by a state church pastor, G. A. Lammers. His study of the Scriptures led him to the conviction that the doctrines of the Lutheran church could not be harmonized with the New Testament. He was particularly disturbed by the doctrines of regeneration in infant baptism and the union of church and state. In 1856 he and several others left the state church and organized an Apostolic Free Church. A number of other "Lammers" churches were established, but a controversy broke out over Lammers's position "that children should not be baptized until they accepted Christ as their personal Saviour, but that those sprinkled in infancy should not be rebaptized."[61] Lammers's church in Skien split on this issue, with one faction forming The Church of the Christian Dissenters in 1858. This was essentially a Baptist church without knowing it was such a church.

It was in this environment and in the nearby community of Porsgrund that a Danish sailor, Fredrik L. Rymker, settled. Rymker had been converted in America and began to do mission work in 1857. He was a simple but dedicated person, well versed in the Scriptures. On December 25, 1858, he baptized a young man named Carl Gunderson Kongeröd. "The first Baptist church was organized on April 22, 1860, at Tolnaes, a farm near Skien, with seven members."[62] Another church was organized the same year at Larvik. In 1861 F. O. Nilsson of Sweden visited Skien and several other places, and in 1862 a third church was established at Kragero. The first Norwegian Baptist minister was Godtfred Hübert who had been baptized in the U.S.A. and served a year in the navy during the Civil War. He returned to Norway in 1862, and for twenty years he was supported by the English

80

Baptists. He established a church at Bergen. Rymker returned to Denmark in 1863.

The Swedish Baptists maintained an interest in the work in Norway. Two of their own pastors, Oluf Larson and O. B. Hansson (better known as Ola Hanson), conducted church work in Norway in 1863. Wiberg in Sweden reported regularly on the work in Norway. In 1866 he wrote:

> A Swedish brother, Ola Hanson from Scania, is now laboring in the Lord's cause in the county of Bradsburg, south of Norway, and, as it seems, through his instrumentality, a church of twenty-five members has lately been organized.[63]

Wiberg made an appeal for help in 1867 for the work in Norway.

> Again and again, letters from Norway, imploring help, have been received. But the great need of laborers in our own country has always limited the visits of our brethren to this field....

> At Conference in August, we had the pleasure of seeing this dear brother, whose name is Ola Hanson, in Stockholm. He is a very earnest, active and zealous young man. In view of the great need in Norway, he said he would not leave Stockholm until a fellow laborer was sent with him....

> In Christiania there is no church, only one family of baptized believers. A church of Mr. Lammers' connection opened their meeting room to Baptist colporteurs.... A few Baptists are also found at Drammen. These however, are not organized into a

church; there is a loud cry for help.[64]

The Baptist work in Norway has not experienced the rapid growth which it had in Sweden in the 1800s. However, there have been some stalwart Norwegian Baptist leaders among whom were J. Jensen, P. Helbostad, A. Milde, G. Nesse, M. A. Öhrn, J. A. Öhrn, Fr. Nilsen, and J. M. Sellevold.

(FINLAND) Two language groups of Baptists developed in Finland--the Swedish-speaking Baptists and the Finnish-speaking Baptists. For over 700 years Sweden ruled Finland, but in 1809 Finland was conquered by Russia and made a Grand Duchy. Consequently, the occupation of the country by two neighboring conquerors is reflected in the population and in languages. The earliest Baptist influence quite naturally developed among the Swedes in Finland.

During the Crimean War, the Aland Islands between Finland and Sweden were occupied by the British fleet the summer of 1855. A Swedish Baptist pastor, C. Möllersvärd, took opportunity to visit the islands then opened by the British. A revival followed, but when the fleet departed, Möllersvärd found it necessary to also leave. But the seed of the gospel had been planted, and Wiberg's book on baptism led three Alanders to visit Stockholm in 1856 to be baptized. One of the three was a customs inspector, G. Fagerström, who was also ordained. Six Baptists then formed a church in Föglo in 1856 [Swedish Baptist reports list the church founding in 1857; Rushbrook reports 1856].

The Baptist movement spread to the mainland of Finland in an interesting manner, and the story was told in 1869. It had its beginning in Aland in 1857:

Some poor persecuted Baptists from the island of Aland were seen walking the

82

streets in the town of Abo [mainland].
They had been summoned to appear before
the consistory of Abo, to answer the
charges of having fallen from the true
evangelical doctrine, and embraced the
heresy of the Anabaptists. Not without
fear (for they did not know whether they
should be banished to Siberia), did they
appear before the consistory. They were
examined, and their case was left to be
decided by higher tribunals. Among
those thus examined was our br. Valin....

As the poor Alanders were leaving the
consistory, Prof. Heikel asked them in a
friendly manner, to call at his house.
They thought, what does it mean? Does
he intend to make some further inquiries,
in order to make the sentence against us
more sure? In calling, however, they
were happily disappointed. The professor
entertained them with food, and treated
them in the most friendly manner. His
children, then young, were witnesses to
all this, and they received a favorable
impression of the Baptists which has
followed them up to the present moment.[65]

We learn that in 1868 the Heikel brother [Viktor]
and sister [Anna] attended the Baptist conference in
Stockholm where they were baptized. They returned to
Finland with evangelistic fervor, converting a number
of their friends. But there was no one to baptize
them until a "brother Valin" appeared in July, 1869.
Valin was one of those Alanders who was questioned
by Prof. Heikel in 1857, and he had since become a
preacher. He was to the mainland converts another
Philip! Anna Heikel described the first mainland
baptism.

The following day, July 14, our friends
were baptized in the forenoon. We were
sitting there in the forest near to the
shore, a small band, unseen by the world,
but not forgotten by Him who says, "Where
two or three are convened in my name,
there I am in the midst of them."
... Thus the first baptism according to
the commandment of Christ had been performed on the shore of Finland.[66]

For a number of years there was no Baptist work
among the Finns. As far as we know, Finnish Baptist
work was begun by a zealous sailor named Henriksson
who had earlier been converted and baptized abroad.
He began to preach to the Finns in 1866, but he died
two years later. One of his converts, Esaias Lund-
berg, picked up Henriksson's work. He established
the first Finnish Baptist church at Loria in 1870.

Rudén and Lahrson, in writing about the work
among the Finnish people in the 1870s, stated:

A Lutheran clergyman, John Hymander,
came to doubt the Lutheran doctrine of
baptism, and resigned from his ministry
in the Lutheran Church. He went to
Stockholm to be baptized, and organized,
after his return, a congregation of baptized believers.[67]

The language differences and differences of
opinion about Baptist organizations resulted in 1903
in the development of separate Baptist conventions
for the Swedish Finns and the Finnish Finns.

Other American Baptist-Related European Work

International Ministries' European Representatives today maintain contact with all of the numerous

European Baptist groups in the previously mentioned countries. However, there are two countries not mentioned in which American Baptists had mission involvement in the 1800s but do not do so today—Greece and Spain. There are two other countries in which we have not engaged in mission—Portugal and Italy. It is beyond the scope of this chapter to present the beginnings of Baptist work in these four countries. Let it suffice to say that American Baptist work in Greece began in 1836 and was discontinued in 1871. In Spain, American Baptist work responsibility, channeled through one missionary, W. I. Knapp, lasted only from 1870 to 1876.

In the 1920 London Conference composed of members of the Baptist World Alliance, representatives of Baptist foreign mission boards, and European Baptist leaders met to consider future relationships for the recovery period following World War I. Some realignments in responsibility were suggested for future foreign mission board/European Baptist relationships and work. Today American Baptist mission relationships in Europe are vastly different from what they were in the 1800s, not so much in philosophy as in funding and fielding personnel.

CHAPTER 3

1. The American Baptist Missionary Magazine (Boston), Vol. 37 (1857), p. 264.
2. Ibid., Vol. 48 (1868), pp. 292-293.
3. Ibid., p. 294.
4. Erik Rudén and Gordon R. Lahrson, Christian Focus on Europe (Valley Forge: American Baptist Foreign Mission Society, 1963), p. 18.
5. J. H. Rushbrooke, The Baptist Movement on the Continent of Europe (London: The Kingsgate Press, 1923), p. 28.
6. Ibid., pp. 28-29.
7. Ibid., pp. 29-30.
8. The American Baptist Missionary Magazine (Boston), Vol. 14 (1833), p. 291.
9. Ibid., Vol. 16 (1836), p. 135.
10. Ibid., Vol. 19 (1838), p. 145.
11. Rushbrooke, op. cit., pp. 32-33.
12. The American Baptist Missionary Magazine (Boston), Vol. 21 (1841), pp. 246-247. (Köbner's letter describes in detail the 1839 visit.)
13. Rushbrooke, op. cit., p. 76.
14. The American Baptist Missionary Magazine (Boston), Vol. 25 (1845), p. 169.
15. Ibid., p. 169.
16. Rushbrooke, op. cit., p. 55.
17. The American Baptist Missionary Magazine (Boston), Vol. 25 (1845), p. 43.
18. Ibid., Vol. 26 (1846), p. 42.
19. Ibid., Vol. 25 (1845), p. 42.
20. Ibid., Vol. 25 (1845), p. 42.
21. Ibid., Vol. 28 (1848), p. 275.
22. Rushbrooke, op. cit., pp. 86-87.
23. The American Baptist Mission Magazine (Boston), Vol. 44 (1864), p. 333.
24. Rushbrooke, op. cit., p. 116.

25. The American Baptist Missionary Magazine
    (Boston), Vol. 25 (1845), p. 42.
26. J. D. Franks, European Baptists Today (Rüsch-
    likon-Zürich: Baublatt, AG, 1952), p. 81.
27. Rushbrooke, op. cit., p. 49.
28. The American Baptist Missionary Magazine
    (Boston), Vol. 35 (1855), p. 326.
29. Ibid., Vol. 41 (1863), p. 263.
30. Rushbrooke, op. cit., p. 50.
31. Ibid., p. 51.
32. The American Baptist Missionary Magazine
    (Boston), Vol. 46 (1866), p. 302.
33. Rushbrooke, op. cit., p. 149.
34. The American Baptist Missionary Magazine
    (Boston), Vol. 40 (1860), p. 264.
35. Erik Rudén and Gordon R. Lahrson, op. cit., p. 61.
36. Rushbrooke, op. cit., p. 158.
37. Ibid., p. 159.
38. Ibid., p. 66.
39. The American Baptist Missionary Magazine
    (Boston), Vol. 38 (1858), pp. 267-268.
40. Rushbrooke, op. cit., p. 65.
41. The American Baptist Missionary Magazine
    (Boston), Vol. 40 (1860), p. 263.
42. Rushbrooke, op. cit., pp. 138-139.
43. Ibid., p. 140.
44. Ibid., p. 131.
45. Ibid., p. 133.
46. The American Baptist Missionary Magazine
    (Boston), Vol. 49 (1869), p. 105.
47. Ibid., Vol. 46 (1866), p. 303.
48. Rushbrooke, op. cit., p. 168.
49. Ibid., p. 169.
50. Rudén and Lahrson, op. cit., p. 79.
51. Rushbrooke, op. cit., p. 69.
52. Ibid., pp. 164-165.
53. Ibid., p. 121.
54. Ibid., p. 108.
55. The American Baptist Missionary Magazine
    (Boston), Vol. 33 (1853), pp. 304-305.

56. <u>Ibid</u>., Vol. 35 (1855), pp. 325–326.
57. <u>Thirty-First Annual Report</u> (Philadelphia: American Baptist Publication Society, 1853), p. 41.
58. <u>Thirty-Seventh Annual Report</u> (Philadelphia: American Baptist Publication Society, 1861), p. 25.
59. <u>The American Baptist Missionary Magazine</u> (Boston), Vol. 46 (1866), p. 308.
60. <u>Ibid</u>., Vol. 61 (1881), p. 264.
61. Rushbrooke, <u>op. cit</u>., p. 102.
62. <u>Ibid</u>., p. 103.
63. <u>The American Baptist Missionary Magazine</u> (Boston), Vol. 46 (1866), p. 423.
64. <u>Ibid</u>., Vol. 62 (1867), pp. 175–176.
65. <u>Ibid</u>., Vol. 51 (1870), p. 285.
66. <u>Ibid</u>., p. 284.
67. Rudén and Lahrson, <u>op. cit</u>., p. 47.

Mrs. Denton (Janice) Lotz
Former BIM Fraternal Representative
Central and Eastern Europe
Washington, D.C.

Mrs. Maurice (Judy) S. Entwistle
BIM Fraternal Representative
Benelux, France, Great Britain
Bruxelles, Belgium

CHAPTER IV

MAGNIFICENT IN STRENGTHENING THE WORK

We have previously discussed European Baptist origins, Baptists under persecution, and how the Baptists expanded between 1832 and 1900. We have tried to see how the work developed during this formative period.

European/American Baptist Relationships

An extremely large and important block of time, 1900-1970, has not been covered. Tremendous changes in Europe occurred during this period. The Baptist work suffered greatly from two World Wars, the Cold War, and continuing East-West tension. During this period American Baptists launched three major financial campaigns which helped to meet some of the European and other overseas fields' Baptist needs:

The New World Movement, 1919-1924.
The World Mission Crusade, 1945-1947.
The World Mission Campaign, 1963-1968.

The combined American Baptist funds from these three campaigns which have been sent to aid European Baptists exceed a million and a half dollars. Among those American Baptist special representatives in Europe who handled major work funds in the past have been W. O. Lewis, Edwin I. Bell, and Gordon R.

EUROPE
in 1914

European Allied States
of World War I

Central States of
World War I

Neutral states

Lahrson.* Probably another million dollars has been
spent during the past ten years in assisting church
building programs, theological schools, scholarships,
and transportation for European Baptist leaders.
Robert G. Torbet has stated:

> Europe has been a unique field among
> those in which the American Baptist For-
> eign Mission Societies have conducted
> missions. With few exceptions, it has
> received from these Societies no mission-
> aries from the United States, only finan-
> cial assistance and friendly counsel.
> In each country where European Baptists
> have received funds from abroad [American
> Baptists'], the principle of acknowledg-
> ing the autonomy of national organiza-
> tions has been observed. Aid has been
> channeled through a special representa-
> tive of the Societies to responsible
> Baptist Unions, churches, or institu-
> tions which handle and disburse the
> monies received with complete freedom
> from outside control.[1]

Torbet's statement regarding the Board's relationship with European Baptists helps us to understand that it truly is "their work." There are four
general areas of strengthening the work which the
annual reports document--finance, organization, program, and theological education. We can best get a
grasp of the voluminous information on these four
topics by focusing attention upon only three groups
of Baptists--those in France, Germany, and Sweden.

---

*Part of the story of Baptist relief and refugee work
has been written by Dana M. Albaugh, Who Shall Separate
Us? (Valley Forge, The Judson Press, 1963).

These are centers from which the Baptist movements expanded throughout Europe.

Financial Undergirding

Although there is no record of a formal Board action showing the adoption of Professor Irah Chase's philosophy for European Baptist support, the Board's practice, to a large degree, evidenced concurrence. Following his exploratory trip to France in 1833, Chase wrote regarding the feasibility of American Baptists beginning mission work there. "The sum necessary to support, for one year, a missionary sent from America, would, if duly managed, educate a native French preacher."[2] We remember that the Board's first missionary appointment to France in 1832 was Casimir Rostan, a Frenchman living in the U.S. at the time. Although a few American Baptist missionaries also have been appointed to France, most of the missionaries have been Frenchmen.

> The Board have appointed the Rev. Antony Porchat, a French Baptist preacher, as their missionary, to be associated with Mr. Willmarth. The Board have also appointed two other French Baptist preachers, as missionaries in France....[3]

The Board appointed all national missionaries in Germany. In Sweden, when the American Baptist Missionary Union took over the work from the American Baptist Publication Society in 1866, all of the missionaries were Swedes; and when additional appointments were made, these also were persons with a Swedish background. The main help in Europe has always been primarily financial, and even this help has been modest until the twentieth century's unusual circumstances. For instance, in 1846 the Board budgeted $3,500 for France and $3,000 for Germany for the support of the missionaries and the work!

The Baptists in Europe during the founding
years were generally from among the poorest peasants.
They came out of a background in which state church
support was mandatory and oppressive. The 1852 Board
report noted: "The people are ready to give...for
almost any other object rather than pastoral support."[4]
The early Baptists suffered physical and psychological
abuse, and often they lost their jobs and their pos-
sessions because of their faith. It took a long time
for the Baptists to make socioeconomic improvement,
to readjust psychologically to the support of a Free
Church ministry, and to build their chapels and
churches.

French Baptists seemed from the beginning to be
in the most difficult financial position. Part of
their difficulty was due to who they were--the poor,
rural, village peasants. This is reflected in annual
report statements by the Board:

> The state of the French mission is ex-
> tremely critical, depending for its exis-
> tence seemingly on Mr. Willard's con-
> nection with it.[5]

> The missionaries have felt embarrassed
> by the frequent discussion of the ques-
> tion whether their work is to be prose-
> cuted or cut off.[6]

> The brethren at Paris were deeply dis-
> tressed on account of the departure of
> Mr. Willard.... The poverty of the pastors,
> and the fear that the mission is to be
> abandoned, have exercised a disheartening
> influence. Several members have emigrated
> to America, including one ordained min-
> ister, and others are seriously contem-
> plating a similar step.[7]

> At the commencement of the financial year,
> notice was communicated to the laborers
> in connection with this mission, that,
> owing to the pressure of the times, and
> in anticipation of the increased diffi-
> culty of raising funds, on account of the
> war in the United States, pecuniary aid
> to the mission must be suspended after
> October 1....[8]

The German Baptist movement, under the dynamic leadership of Oncken and a number of exceedingly capable leaders, was able to secure outside financial support in non-crippling, non-dependency ways. Oncken's fluency in English and his wide contacts in Scotland, England, and the United States gave him access to centers of denominational resources and to many interested Baptists. He made a number of trips abroad to raise funds. The Board report for 1868 noted that the current work support in Germany came from three main sources:

> Contributions from friends in Great
> Britain. $6,000
>
> Appropriations from American Baptist
> Mission Union (for preachers and col-
> porteurs). $1,850
>
> Contributions from the German
> churches $1,500

In 1875 when the Board was further cutting back support for Germany, it was noted:

> A large number of churches formerly
> aided in that country have become self-
> supporting; and many of those still
> aided are helped by funds raised by Mr.
> Oncken in England. A large number of

evangelists are also sustained by the contribution of funds in this country [U.S.] and in Europe, independently of any society....

There never was a time when a large portion of the funds placed at the disposal of Mr. Oncken and the German committee was not furnished by persons having no special relation to us....

In short, the aid given by this society was the nucleus, and it has been the steadiest nourishment of the work among the Germans. But the time has come when it is neither necessary nor wise for the old relations to continue; and, while we do not withdraw all aid and counsel, it is no longer possible to maintain the exact status of former years.[9]

Oncken prodded the churches in Germany to support missions and to be missionary. Within fifteen years of the beginning of Baptist work in Germany, the Hamburg church [Oncken's] was supporting three missionaries, paid for a place of worship [an old warehouse], raised annually $300 for the poor, and contributed to various tract and Bible societies. Furthermore, a number of other churches were doing the same thing. Interestingly, thirty years after Oncken started the Hamburg church it was still meeting in the warehouse, but he had raised funds from various sources to build more than twenty chapels.

Several of the Bible and Tract Societies, especially in Great Britain, made significant financial contributions to the Baptist work in Europe. The British and Foreign Bible Society, as previously mentioned, was extremely helpful in the expansion of the German Baptist movement throughout Europe. In the year of Oncken's death, 1883, the Board recognized the importance of the financial assistance which had been given by just one agency.

> The National Bible Society of Scotland, whose agent Mr. Oncken had been for over fifty years, has met Dr. Bickely with the same confidence, and retained him as their agent for the work in Germany. In this way he is enabled to engage about twenty-five men as colporteurs for the society. Most of these men are Baptists.

> ... The Bible Society pays each man a certain sum as a fixed salary; and, if they are Baptists, the churches in whose territory they labor pay an equal amount. Our work is thus indirectly supported by the National Bible Society of Scotland, to an amount not much below what is given by the Baptists.[10]

Organizational Development

Most Baptist readers today give little thought to denominational organizations. Such organizations are taken for granted, many of them having been around for several hundred years. However, it is different when a new denomination begins in a country, such as was the situation with the Baptists in Europe. Each new church had to struggle first in getting itself established. Only later were needs felt for cooperative endeavors, a wider systematized fellowship, institutions and publications, and church planning and planting. Studying the nineteenth century development of Baptist churches in Europe sheds light upon organizational development.

(FRANCE) By 1838 Mr. Willard noted the need

for bringing together in some manner little churches
which were so scattered as to make visitation difficult. He said if he had an associate, one of them
could itinerate among the churches. In 1847 he reported that "The native laborers have organized themselves into an Association or Conference. They have
also formed a society for the publication of Baptist
books and tracts."[11] They had also begun to establish principles of faith and order, discipline, and
had begun to cooperate with each other. This led in
1849 to the formation of the first Baptist Association composed of 15 churches. This was followed
shortly thereafter by the forming of a Ministers'
Conference.

The next organizational concern appeared to be
how to organize more effectively in order to carry
out Baptist work which was scattered in the north
and south of France, as well as in parts of Belgium
and Switzerland. The answer was to divide the work
into the Department of the North [north of Paris
and Belgium] and the Department of the South [south
of Paris and in Switzerland]. This was done in
1850, some 28 years after the work had begun.

For a number of years, the French mission de-
pended heavily upon Willard, both financially and
administratively. After he left France in 1856,
pleas came to the Board for a replacement American
missionary. The Board sent a letter to the French
Mission in 1865 stating:

> However useful, and even necessary,
> Americans may have been in the early
> stages of the mission, the Committee
> do not see sufficient reason to return
> to that dispensation. They want you to
> try the New Testament plan. Be your own
> bishops and superintendents. In other
> words, be Baptists in all respects, in

accordance with the teachings of the
Scriptures. You can in no other way
gain strength as you should.[12]

(GERMANY)   Oncken's organizational skills may
be partly attributed to his work with Bible and tract
societies. These skills were also utilized in the
Hamburg church and in all his Baptist work in Europe.
We shall read more about this under the section on
"Program Development." In 1845 he wrote: "A number
of our female members were formed recently into a
society for the purpose of lending tracts and supplying the people with the scriptures. I am to meet
with these sisters once a month."[13] A year later he
reported:

> The Hamburg "Young Men's Union," under
> the superintendence of Mr. C. Schauffler,
> is growing in importance. More than
> forty brethren have been sent out from
> it into every part of Germany, and the
> demand for additional laborers from all
> quarters, is constantly increasing.[14]

In 1848 Lehmann, a colleague of Oncken, called
together in Berlin representatives from the Baptist
churches in Prussia. They organized themselves into
an Association. Rushbrooke pointed to two other
significant decisions coming out of the Berlin meeting.

> The first was that 2/3rds of the total
> contribution should be applied locally,
> and 1/3rd should be transmitted to the
> American Board for foreign mission work....
> The other decision appointed Wilheim
> Weist as the first itinerant missionary
> within the area of the associated churches
> to devote himself to the founding of the
> new stations.[15]

I did not find a record of how long these decisions may have been carried out, but their significance is worth noting because it expresses the German Baptist mission concern outreach.

One year after the formation of the Prussian Association, 1849, fifty-six representatives from the Baptist churches in Germany and Denmark gathered in Hamburg where they organized the Union of Associated Churches of Baptized Christians in Germany and Denmark. The Union, patterned after the American Baptist Missionary Union, was to meet triennially. The Union had four subdivisions or Associations: the Prussian Association with Berlin as its center; the Association of North Western Germany with Hamburg as its center; the Association of Middle and Southern Germany with Eimbeck as its center; and the Danish Association with Copenhagen as its center. The representatives defined the purposes of the Union.

(1) Confession (a confession of faith prepared by Oncken, Köbner, and Lehmann was adopted).
(2) Strengthen Baptist fellowship.
(3) Promote missionary activity.
(4) Prepare statistical information.[16]

Five years after the formation of the Union, and after Oncken had been in the United States to raise money, the Board sanctioned in 1854 the formal organization of the German Mission consisting of Oncken, Lehmann, Schauffler, Köbner, and Braun. Triennial meetings were held in Hamburg so long as Oncken lived, in recognition of his great influence. But the Baptists in the later years began to get restless about the place of the Triennial meetings, and we find in the German Mission report to the Board in 1886:

> The meeting of our churches [was] held in Berlin.... Never before have our churches

convened anywhere else for their triennial
gatherings than at Hamburg. Some were
therefore beginning to look upon Hamburg
as a Baptistic Jerusalem, or a Mohammedan
Mecca, to which Baptists must make a pilgrimage from time to time. A meeting outside of Hamburg was beginning to be felt
to be a necessary thing.[17]

(The Danish Baptist churches had formed their own
conference in 1866 to which Oncken and Köbner had
been invited.)

(SWEDEN)   The Swedish Mission was no doubt influenced by the German Mission in matters of organization. The Stockholm Missionary Union was established in 1857. In the same year, a Conference of
Swedish Baptists was called to which "nineteen delegates gathered from eight provinces, and all reported
encouraging progress. Sunday schools had already
been started. It was decided to organize the work
under a central committee."[18] In 1858 and 1861 subsequent conferences were called. During the latter
meeting, it was decided to instruct the Executive
Committee to "establish a school for the education
of preachers." Wiberg then spent three years [1863-
1866] in the U.S.A. raising money for the new chapel
in Stockholm. When he returned he brought K. O.
Broady whom the American Baptist Missionary Union
had appointed to found the seminary.

Other organized efforts followed in the 1870s.
A brother Wingren living in Kristianstad in the south
of Sweden developed a system of day schools, using
volunteer help—primarily females whom he instructed.
This was a copy of an earlier work begun in northern
Sweden. "Besides this enterprise, br. W. [Wingren]
has also begun to organize systematic mission efforts
for the spread of the gospel through his part of the
country."[19]

There were several missionary organizations developed in addition to the Stockholm Missionary Union. There was the Sundsvall Missionary Union and the Wendes Missionary Union. It was not long before a certain amount of competition for funds developed. One of the early attempts to reduce competition and confusion was initiated by the Stockholm Missionary Union in 1870.

> The members of "The Stockholm Missionary Union" who were present, informed the Conference that this Union had changed its Constitution, so that it now is a Baptist Missionary Society, and recommended it to the sympathy of the Baptist churches in the country in general, at the same time expressly declaring that the object was not to supplant other local Missionary Societies, but to collect missionary resources which otherwise would be lost.[20]

It was not until 1873 that the Conference was able to form a Foreign Mission Society. The next organizational step occurred in 1889 when the Swedish Baptist Union was formed.

> In 1889 a change was made in the organization of the Union, so that each branch of the work should be entrusted to a special committee. Thus there arose committees for foreign missions, home missions, publications, chapel buildings, and Sunday schools, the executive committee of the Union being composed of the members of the other committees. (This system worked well until 1914 when it was again changed.)[21]

Generally, Baptist organizational development in other European countries in the 1800s followed, with modifications and some variances, that which took place in France, Germany, and Sweden. Organizational patterns tended to be similar to those of the Baptists who first came into their countries from other countries.

Program Development

It is not possible from the limited English records to discover the extent of program development among European Baptists. In the earlier years in each country the primary concern was evangelism. Only later did Christian nurture and service activities of a more distinct and organized character begin to emerge.

Colporteuring and Publishing: Throughout the 1800s, tract and Scripture distribution was one of the highest priorities among European Baptists. The colporteur system, or perhaps more accurately, colporteurs paved the way for church establishment. As early as 1836, Willard wrote from France, "I think good could be effected here by the circulation of tracts and by the sale of Scriptures, or by the gratuitous distribution of them."[22] He went on in his letter to indicate that he had received some from Paris, but they were not attractive or of good quality. Two years later, Willard noted that

> The number of native preachers being wholly inadequate to supply the destitution already laid open to the missionaries, the colporting system, in addition to its intrinsic merits, is commended to us by the necessities of the case.[23]

It was Oncken who was outstanding in his use of tracts and the colporteur system, he himself being a colporteur of a tract society and later the National

Bible Society of Scotland. As early as 1836, we read of Oncken visiting ships in the port of Hamburg "supplying them with the Word of Life." The Board appointed Lange in 1836 as a colporteur, or Bible and tract distributor. In 1839 we read in the Board report that:

> The circulation of the holy scriptures
> has received a new and powerful impulse,
> through the liberal grants of money from
> the American and the Foreign Bible Societies.... A considerable number of
> scriptures have been sold and distributed
> among seamen visiting this port [Hamburg],
> in the Danish, Dutch, French, Spanish,
> and Swedish languages. Emigrants to
> various parts of the world have also
> been supplied with the word of God....
> We have issued from our society 16 different tracts, 13 in German, and 3 in
> the Danish language; amounting in all to
> 193,000 copies; besides these, we received
> from other societies 70,000 copies, making
> in all 263,000, of which 240,000 have been
> distributed during 1837-1838.[24]

Oncken was not satisfied simply to be a tract and Bible distributor. He became a publisher, and he founded a great printing establishment which he eventually bequeathed to the German Baptist Union in 1883 or 1884. (We know from the 1884 Board report that the Publication Society in Philadelphia sent a Dr. Bickel to take charge of the publishing business which was at that time not paying its own way.)

Perhaps the first regular Baptist journal in Europe was started by Oncken in 1848. It was called Das Missionsblatt. In 1847 France had formed a publication society for Baptist books and tracts, but nothing more is reported for years. In Sweden the

Stockholm Missionary Union was also a publication society. It was perhaps the second oldest European Baptist publishing agency. It was formed in 1856, and thirteen years later [1869] "it had issued about 1,362,000 copies of books and tracts, amounting to 11,690,000 pages."[25] In 1879 the French Baptists began to publish a monthly paper, L'Echo de la Verité.

The Sunday school was first introduced on the Continent in 1825 by Oncken, ten years before he had been appointed a Baptist missionary. However, Sunday schools never received a great push in the Baptist churches in Germany. Oncken had too many other interests to which he gave higher priority. For instance, in 1884, the year Oncken died, German Baptists had 157 churches and 1,490 preaching stations but only 421 Sunday schools. The church membership was 32,293 whereas Sunday school enrollment was 15,585.

We have previously mentioned the development of missionary societies in Sweden, but perhaps the earliest such organizations were in Germany. As early as 1851, there is recorded in the German Mission report: "The female missionary association has circulated 937 copies of the Scripture and 17,688 tracts, and has collected for missionary purposes 205 marks one shilling."[26] Two years later, another reference is made to "The Female Association" composed of "young women." The latter "has supported a brother in laboring two days a week for the ten thousand Jews in Hamburg."[27] They also supplied clothing to needy children in the Sabbath school. The German Baptists sent Mr. C. Bäschlin as their missionary to China in 1870.

Although French Baptists had to struggle from the beginning, there is at least one reference to a mission organization. The following statement appeared in the French Mission report for 1881.

During the year the Woman's Baptist Missionary Society has taken into its employ Mlle. E. M. Crétin, daughter of the pastor at La Fère, who will labor as a general missionary among the women and children, in connection with the Church at Paris.[28]

There are other programs, such as youth work and scouting, to which only allusions are made in the English records. The latter program has been especially effective in Scandinavia. Rushbrooke, in 1923, referred to the "deaconness movement," but he did not give it a time frame. (We know that in 1963 the movement had 900 deaconesses, six hospitals, and fifteen to twenty homes and social institutions related to the Baptists in East and West Germany.)

Pastor Training

European Baptists realized very early that some form of pastoral training would be needed. The future of the Baptist movement in each country would to a large degree become dependent upon competent and dedicated leaders--persons who could give most of their time to evangelizing, educating, and developing the churches. In the earliest years such training was done informally in an apprentice-type relationship with recognized leaders. Oncken was perhaps the greatest of the European Baptist leaders who could spot persons of high leadership potential, train them in a work situation, inspire them, and develop a loyalty with them that few other persons have ever been able to accomplish. But it was not in Germany that the first formal and substantive theological education took place. That honor belongs to Sweden.

When Wiberg returned to Sweden in 1866 after his second trip to the United States, he was accompanied by a man who was eventually to become his successor

as the leader of the Swedish Baptist work—a man who
was to have a tremendous impact upon Swedish Baptists
for fifty-seven years. Rushbrooke tells the story
succinctly:

> K. O. Broady...had been sent back to his
> native land by the American Baptist Mis-
> sion Society, for the purpose of founding
> a seminary. Mr. Broady (afterwards Dr.),
> though a Swede by birth, was converted and
> acquired his theological education in
> America. He proved a man of sterling
> character, and of exceptional gifts as a
> teacher and preacher.... Dr. Broady re-
> mained for 40 years its president [1866-
> 1906] and continued to teach in the in-
> stitution for another 17 years until his
> death in 1922, at the age of 90.[29]

Broady reported to the American Baptist Missionary Union in 1867:

> Our contemplated Literary and Theological
> Institute was successfully conceived and
> begotten, and was named "The Swedish Bethel
> Seminary." Thirteen of the most influ-
> ential brethren from the different churches,
> together with the Faculty of the school,
> were elected a corporate body. A Consti-
> tution was framed and adopted. It is
> liberal in spirit, offering the advantages
> of the school to all, irrespective of
> creed, whoever might choose to pay the
> limited sum of Rex. 40, about $10. It
> was thought necessary to put the tuition
> at this low figure, because the people,
> as a class, are extremely poor....
>
> The Corporation went to work without de-
> lay, and elected brn. G. Palmquist, Drake,

Edgren, Wiberg and Broady as teachers.
G. Palmquist takes the rudimentary
branches; Drake, the Historical and
Greek; Edgren, the Mathematical and
Scientific; and Broady, the Theological
and English. Br. Wiberg teaches what
and when he chooses....

Our school rooms at present are in the
basement of the new church edifice. We
opened the school on the 1st of October,
and began with seven scholars....

We have divided the academical year into
two terms, the first beginning with August
and ending at Christmas; the second beginning in the latter part of January and
ending with the close of May. We study
five days in the week.[30]

The school was not without problems, some short-
term and others long-range. First of all, in common
with general European Baptist feelings about theological education, there was a widespread lay skepti-
cism and aversion to "training men of God"! This
was in reaction to the state church deadness and
ministers who were only functionaries. "In many
minds exists a decided aversion to an educated ministry, it being looked upon as being equivalent to a
godless ministry."[31] These are Broady's words.

Apparently very soon after the opening of the
seminary, there developed a split. G. Palmquist,
one of the seminary teachers, started a Bible school.
The seminary's academic standards and scope of curriculum excluded the Bible school-type students who
were looked upon more favorably by many Baptists.
In other words, Broady's beginning seemed to be too
academic and scholarly. This frightened the older
partially-trained pastors in the churches. The

The Bethel Seminary, Stockholm, Sweden. This is the first Baptist theological seminary established in Europe. American Baptists helped in the earlier days.

The People's High School (sometimes called Folk School), Töllöse, Denmark, a unique Scandinavian institution which provides for laymen some orientation in church history, polity, music, and teaching skills on a six-month basis.

Foreign Secretary for Europe visited the field in 1867, discovered the situation, and brought the representatives of the two schools together in conference.

> The representatives of both parties came together, and, after many hours of careful inquiry and deliberation, it was decided without a dissenting voice, that the two schools should be merged into one, with a regular and partial course of study; and that Gustavus Palmquist should be principal teacher in the partial course. This plan has since been carried out in all except the last feature. In that respect death interposed to thwart our plans.[32]

French Baptists were to have to wait until 1880 before they had a regularly organized Baptist Theological School. However, very early in the French Mission, American Baptist missionaries Willmarth and Willard provided several students with informal instruction for the ministry. In 1836 their letters revealed that they were teaching Cretin, Caulier, Moutel, and Pruvots--some of the men who later became strong leaders. Willard referred to this type of instruction as "The Prophets' School."

Sometime around 1850 there developed the Douai School for Assistants which was really a continuation of The Prophets' School.

> The object of chief interest at Douai was the school for native preachers. The pupils, now numbering four, one of them an assistant in the literary department, are young men of good native endowments, eager for knowledge, and of apparently sincere and ardent piety....

The duties connected with this institution have engrossed necessarily a large share of Mr. Willard's time and attention. The studies have been various in kind, having regard both to literary and theological training, and have demanded on the part of the teacher thorough and exact preparation—more especially in the critical interpretation of the Scriptures, and not excepting the duties belonging to the pastoral office and the constituting and upbuilding of Christian churches.... Mr. Willard is a thorough scholar, well versed in the science of biblical interpretation....[33]

German Baptist theological education was for many years carried on by Oncken and Köbner on an occasional short-term basis. By 1849 they were conducting six-month training courses, operating from November to May. One problem was finance, so the matter was brought to the attention of the 1851 Triennial meeting. The cost per student was only $1.75 per week, but there were twenty or more students. It was recommended that the churches share in the cost of the school. Theological education continued along this line for a number of years.

In 1867 the Foreign Secretary for Europe visited Germany. In his report to the Board he stated:

It was plain to see that Mr. Oncken is not prepared at once to throw himself into a movement of this kind. If the measure had, in times past, received the approval of his judgment, accompanied with such action as he is accustomed to bestow on whatever he undertakes, a school would ere this have been in existence. Other and in his judgment more important, enterprises have pressed upon him in quick suc-

cession, crowding this into a future day.
The example of learning without piety, in
the pulpit, has constantly been before him
and exerted its inevitable influence.
From the first, he has insisted on these
four qualities in the preacher; he must
be taught by the Holy Spirit, in other
words, be a truly converted man; he must
recognize a distinct call of God to this
service; he must have common sense; he
must really preach, i.e., have power to
interest people sufficiently to gain a
hearing. Of such, scores and scores have
risen up in different quarters, and from
all occupations in life; and these, dis-
ciplined by trial, and improved by reading the Word of God and prayer, are the
men now occupying the more important as
well as less prominent places in the
land. On several occasions, at intervals
of three or four years, classes have been
gathered at Hamburg, and they have spent
six months in study under the tuition of
such men as Oncken, Köbner, Braun, and
the younger Lehmann. The general opinion
is that something more formal and thorough-
going is demanded, and must before long
be attempted.[34]

Theological education continued along the lines
outlined by the Foreign Secretary until 1879 when
the German Baptist Union voted to reopen the Biblical
School in Hamburg which had been closed a few years
due to a controversy between the Hamburg and Altona
church which involved Oncken. The Biblical School
reopened in 1880 with Mr. Moritz Geiszler as professor. Money flowed in from the German churches
and from sources abroad to support the school. By
1888 the Board report recorded:

Since its opening as a permanent institution in the fall of 1880, thirty-five
brethren have enjoyed its benefits: fifteen of them for a short course; twenty
for a full course, which at first extended
over three years, but was changed in
April, 1883, into a four-year course....

So there are twenty-four young men in our
theological school at present, preparing
for a great work. According to nationalities, these are, one Dutchman, two
Swiss, one Austrian, one Lithuanian, one
Russian, two German-Russians, and eighteen
are Germans.[35]

European Baptists so well strengthened their
work during the mid and late 1800s that they could
withstand the terrible pressures and destruction
which would become their lot in the 1900s. The remaining chapters will indicate something of their
contemporary witness and work.

The Baptist Theological Seminary library, Töllöse, Denmark, made possible through
International Ministries and other financial assistance.

CHAPTER 4

1. Robert G. Torbet, Venture of Faith (Philadelphia: The Judson Press, 1955), p. 580.
2. The American Baptist Missionary Magazine (Boston), Vol. 13 (1893), p. 335.
3. Ibid., Vol. 16 (1835), p. 299.
4. Ibid., Vol. 32 (1852), p. 289.
5. Ibid., Vol. 20 (1839), p. 131.
6. Ibid., Vol. 34 (1853), p. 312.
7. Ibid., Vol. 38 (1857), p. 267.
8. Ibid., Vol. 42 (1862), p. 301.
9. Ibid., Vol. 56 (1875), p. 266.
10. Ibid., Vol. 64 (1884), p. 286.
11. Ibid., Vol. 27 (1847), p. 252.
12. Ibid., Vol. 45 (1865), pp. 268-269.
13. Ibid., Vol. 25 (1845), p. 41.
14. Ibid., Vol. 26 (1846), p. 202.
]5. J. H. Rushbrooke, The Baptist Movement in the Continent of Europe (London: The Kingsgate Press, 1923), p. 36.
16. The American Baptist Missionary Magazine (Boston), Vol. 29 (1849), p. 37.
17. Ibid., Vol. 67 (1886), p. 302.
18. Rushbrooke, op. cit., p. 93.
19. The American Baptist Missionary Magazine (Boston), Vol. 50 (1870), p. 276.
20. Ibid., p. 281.
21. Rushbrooke, op. cit., p. 95.
22. The American Baptist Missionary Magazine (Boston), Vol. 16 (1836), p. 298.
23. Ibid., Vol. 18 (1838), p. 144.
24. Ibid., Vol. 19 (1839), p. 131.
25. Ibid., Vol. 50 (1870), p. 282.
26. Ibid., Vol. 32 (1851), p. 296.
27. Ibid., Vol. 33 (1853), p. 306.
28. Ibid., Vol. 61 (1881), p. 257.
29. Rushbrooke, op. cit., p. 94.

30. The American Baptist Missionary Magazine (Boston), Vol. 48 (1867), p. 314.
31. Ibid., Vol. 50 (1869), p. 283.
32. Ibid., Vol. 48 (1868), p. 287.
33. Ibid., Vol. 32 (1852), p. 280.
34. Ibid., Vol. 48 (1868), p. 284.
35. Ibid., Vol. 68 (1888), p. 297.

An open air baptism at Tranas, Sweden. In the early years of the Baptist movement in Scandinavia, baptisms were often performed in secrecy.

CHAPTER 5

MAGNIFICENT IN COOPERATIVE BAPTIST ENDEAVORS

EUROPEAN BAPTIST FEDERATION
C. Ronald Goulding

Beginning and Early Development

There are few land areas comparable in size to Europe which have so many frontiers and causes of division and yet can claim a basic unity. De Gaulle's famous statement about the unity of a Europe stretching from the Atlantic to the Urals embodies a fundamental fact. The roots of European unity lie deep in the distinctive civilization which for good and ill has been predominantly moved by "Christianity." However, any reference to Christian Europe must be purely nostalgic although the phrase sometimes now used of "post-Christian Europe" is too dramatic. Certainly any attempt to build the unity of Europe today by nostalgic reference to the past would be unrealistic and therefore foolish. Technology, modern communications, and the mass media are the major contemporary instruments for forging such a unity. Yet this does not mean that the churches as institutions and Christians as individuals have no part to play.

Indeed it is in the area of unifying a divided

115

people beyond the frontiers of political and social division that the Christian church has made its most significant progress and in this progress Baptists have played and are playing a significant part.

The Roman Empire once provided political unity in the Mediterranean world and northward through Europe as far as England. Trading and cultural exchange flourished. After the Germanic invasions, however, Europe was fragmented. People settled down within the walls of castles and cities and behind geographical barriers such as rivers and mountains. Cultural and linguistic differences and geographically restricted loyalties developed. Still, there was a certain unity in Europe—the unity of Christendom. The Roman popes claimed temporal powers much as the Caesars did. Even when these could not be asserted, the papacy had great "spiritual" powers; for the period of the Middle Ages was a time of faith and superstition. Roman Catholic faith and practice bound western Europe together.

With the growth of modern national states, men began to think of themselves as Englishmen, Frenchmen, Spaniards. National interests frequently clashed; ambitions and rivalries led to war. The first half of the twentieth century tragically witnessed two world wars both of which started in Europe.

The first Christian church in Europe was founded in Philippi, Macedonia, in the first century when Paul and his companions answered the call of the "man of Macedonia." Apart from the fact that the foundation witness of this church was a conversion experience and public baptism, there is no trace of what could rightly be called a "Baptist movement" until the Reformation and the rise of the Anabaptists.

The Anabaptist movement spread rapidly all over

116

Central Europe; and what might have happened if the Anabaptists had not been so terribly persecuted, we can only speculate. Certainly any form of Baptist movement was very nearly extinguished.

The fragments were gathered together in freedom-loving Holland, and from Holland the living center of the movement passed to England, spreading to America and later to the rest of the world.

Nearly two centuries passed before the movement in Europe came to life again. The new beginning dates from 1834 when Johann Gerhard Oncken was baptized in the River Elbe at Hamburg, Germany, together with his wife and five other believers. The next day a Baptist church was founded. Oncken was a great God-given apostle to Europe and his name must always be held in the highest esteem among the great missionary church planters in our Baptist history.

Oncken's example was followed soon afterwards by two other great leaders, Julius Köbner in 1836 and Gottfried Lehmann in 1837. These three men were a remarkable triumvirate and under their guidance and inspired leadership the Baptist movement spread far and wide and within one hundred years had penetrated Europe.

With the growth came persecution, and in many countries Baptist believers had to suffer and endure great hardship. Many were imprisoned and exiled for their faith. Such growth as there was should be understood against the background of state church opposition, political interference and restriction with a resulting attitude on the part of European society generally to regard "Baptists" more as an obscure sect, rather than a serious part of the Christian church--an attitude which still persists today.

Although the witness increased, Baptists lived generally in national isolation. Language problems, cultural differences, and two world wars were generally responsible for this.

IN 1949 THE MOST SIGNIFICANT STEP IN THE UNIFYING OF BAPTIST LIFE IN EUROPE TOOK PLACE IN THE BEGINNING OF THE FORMATION OF THE EUROPEAN BAPTIST FEDERATION.

This period also marks another most significant step in the unifying of European Baptist life. In 1948 the Foreign Mission Board of the Southern Baptist Convention set up an institution in Rüschlikon, Zürich, Switzerland, to train men for the Baptist ministry in Europe. The seminary brought students

The 1979 inauguration of SITE (Summer Institute of Theological Education), Rüschlikon, Switzerland. L to R, Dr. Denton Lotz, originator of SITE; Dr. Gerhard Claas, former General Secretary of the European Baptist Federation, now General Secretary of the Baptist World Alliance.

from their national environments and trained them
side by side. Thus wherever they came from and
wherever they settled, they became part of a common
European family in the service of the gospel of
Christ Jesus. Many came from countries whose governments had but a few years earlier been engaged in
the 1939-1945 World War II. Thus was dramatic reconciliation effected.

Although these two outstanding events so closely
related in time and purpose were the outstanding
landmarks in building a unified Baptist life in Europe, there had been a number of other events which
helped to prepare the ground.

When Baptists representing twenty-three countries met together in 1905 and formed the Baptist

SITE's 1980 faculty and students from Switzerland, Romania, Great Britain, Czechoslovakia, Yugoslavia, Denmark, German Democratic Republic, Spain, Portugal, Hungary, Italy, Federal Republic of Germany, Egypt, and the U.S.A.

World Alliance, it was in London, England, that the meeting took place. It was in Europe that the first Congress was held, and five of the 14 World Congresses have been held in Europe.

The seeking for a reality in the unity of European Baptist life led to two European Congresses being held in Berlin in 1908 and in Stockholm in 1913.

In 1920 a meeting which was claimed as the most important in the history of European Baptists up to that time was held in London. It was called by the Executive Committee of the Baptist World Alliance. Its purpose was to plan for cooperation in regard to relief work, rebuilding of churches, and building more theological institutions. Besides the U.S.A. and Canada, 18 European countries were represented. At this meeting the Continent was divided into three areas each of which should be supported in a fraternal relationship by the American Baptist Societies, the Baptists of Canada and Great Britain, and by the stronger European Baptist Unions.

In this period a great deal of healing reconciliation was accomplished. Then came the 1939-1945 war, and it seemed that all the good that had been done would be shattered and destroyed by the destruction caused and the animosity and hatred engendered.

When the war ended and the lights began to flicker on again amidst the rubble and ruin of cities, towns, villages, and churches, it was found that there were in Baptist life still men and women of courage, faith, and vision who began a ministry of reconciliation and healing.

As the writer to the Hebrews says in his own defense: "Time would fail me to tell of...." (Hebrews 11:32); so this story must do likewise and refer to them in general terms.

As in 1920 so again in 1948 a conference was called by the Baptist World Alliance in London. At this meeting a Committee of Seven was set up to devise and create a scheme "for the closer integration of European Baptists." In Rüschlikon, Switzerland, on October 9, 1949, this committee met at the Baptist Theological Seminary and drew up a constitution and plan for a "European Baptist Federation." The outcome of their work was the formation of the Federation at a meeting held at 48, Rue de Lille, Paris, France, on Friday and Saturday, October 20 and 21, 1950.[1] Ten Baptist Unions were represented at this meeting, and they were joined by Rev. W. O. Lewis representing the Baptist World Alliance.

The Committee of Seven accepted the constitution with only minor changes, and the first election of officers took place. W. O. Lewis was elected "temporary chairman."

Dr. Bredahl Petersen of Denmark was elected President; Henry Cook of the Baptist Union of Great Britain and Ireland, Vice-President; and W. O. Lewis Secretary/Treasurer pro temporis. Following the election Dr. Petersen immediately took the chair. At this meeting an Executive Committee was appointed also, and the following brethren were called upon to serve: A. A. Hardenberg, Netherlands; Hans Luckey, Germany; Manfredi Ronchi, Italy; and Henri Vincent, France.

The meeting immediately went to work. The next meeting was called for August 2-6, 1951, in Hamburg, and dates for the first all-European Congress of the Federation were accepted. It was planned to be held in Copenhagen, Denmark, for July 29-August 3, 1952.[2]

Among other decisions which were made, the following give some indication of the way in which the work of the Federation could and indeed did develop.

These comments are taken verbatim from the minutes of the first meeting of the Federation.

The President suggested that various commissions should be set up and that the possibility of opening new work in certain places where there is no Baptist work should be explored.

The following objects should have priority for the next few years:

a. The building of an Oncken Memorial Church in Hamburg as an expression of European Baptist unity.

b. In view of the importance of Strasbourg as headquarters of the Council of Europe, a serious effort should be made to establish a Baptist work in that city. It was felt first of all a worker with a knowledge of French and German should be found and put to work on this field. The French and Swiss Baptists should take the lead in finding such a man, and the Baptists of Europe and America should be asked to provide funds for his support for the next few years.

c. In view of opportunities now existing in Spain, it was felt that the Baptists in Hispanic America should be urged to enter these doors.

d. Having heard from A. K. Dahl the account of the progress in securing a site for a theological school in Oslo, Norway, and having learned that the American Baptist Foreign Mission

122

Society[3] is willing to provide dollars
for this school up to $50,000, it was
agreed that the Baptists of Europe
should be urged to make contributions
to help Norwegian Baptists to complete
this project.

e. After discussion of the needs of the
Finnish-speaking Baptists in Finland,[4]
it was agreed to refer this matter
for advice to the Scandinavian Baptist
Council. It was agreed that a Finnish
hymn book is needed.

All of these projects were accomplished in due time.

Also at this meeting it was agreed that the
Federation should issue a newssheet, and Henry Cook
was appointed to gather news and send out such a
newsletter.

This was an attempt to cross the division lines
in Europe and to create a new interest and concern
at local/national level among Baptists for each other.
Like all of the early Federation projects it suffered
from lack of funds, and much of what was accomplished
was due to the work of Henry Cook and financial support he was able to raise personally.

Something of the "poverty line" financial position of the early development period can be judged
from the budget of the Federation for 1960 which
reads:

Projects (special and continuing-- including Belgium and Finland)	$ 14,500
Youth projects	650
Share of office expenses	1,400
Travel (Executive and Secretary)	2,000
Contingencies	450
	$ 19,000

Influences in the Development of the European Baptist Federation

From the beginning of the formation of the European Baptist Federation and indeed much earlier than the formation, the influence in interest and practical support of Baptists outside of the European continent are obvious.

Baptist World Alliance: Historically would come the Baptist World Alliance which from its foundation in London, England, in 1905 has been most closely linked with Europe. Indeed up until 1941 the headquarters of the Alliance was in London and was only then moved because of the danger of destruction by bombing.

The headquarters was moved to Washington, D.C., U.S.A., and a European office of the Alliance was maintained in the building of the Baptist Union of Great Britain and Ireland at No. 4 Southampton Row, London, until 1976 when it was transferred to Hamburg, Germany. It was further moved to Copenhagen, Denmark, in 1980 where it is located at Lärdalsgade 7.

It was not merely the fact that an office was located in Europe that proved such an influence, but that the Baptist World Alliance permitted its European Associate Secretary also to be Secretary/Treasurer of the Federation. In this way the European Baptist Federation Secretary was supplied by the Alliance as was the office and the assistant to the Secretary also. Without this substantial practical and financial aid it is difficult to see how the Federation could have been started or survived.

There have been five General Secretaries,[5] and at present this office is held by the Rev. Knud Wümpelmann who was until 1980 the General Secretary

124

of the Baptist Union of Denmark.

Dr. Josef Nordenhaug as then Secretary of the Baptist World Alliance, wrote in the European Baptist in November 1964:

> Among the functions of the European Baptist Federation is the furtherance of the aims and objectives of the Baptist World Alliance so far as these affect the life of Baptist churches in Europe.
>
> Since the organization of the European Baptist Federation, the sense of unity of the European Baptists has increased; and they have undertaken certain projects together in which they have sought to add their common strength to places where the Baptist work is facing problems.

It should perhaps be added that the influence has not been altogether one way. In 1980 the Secretary/Treasurer of the European Baptist Federation, Dr. Gerhard Claas, was called to leave Europe to become the Executive Secretary of the Baptist World Alliance. He thus became the third European to have undertaken that office following Dr. Arnold Ohrn (Norway) and Dr. Josef Nordenhaug (Norway).

American Baptist Churches' International Ministries: It could be argued that the American Baptist Churches in the U.S.A. took the initiative in founding Baptist work in Europe insofar as it was one of their members, Professor Barnas Sears of Hamilton College, traveled to Europe to baptize Oncken in Hamburg.

American Baptist interest has been constantly expressed in European Baptists from the earliest days and particularly since the foundation of the Federation.

SITE—Mini-libraries are presented to the 1980 students. These books are deeply appreciated by pastors who often do not have the hard currency required to buy Western theological books.

Baptist leaders from Estonia and Yugoslavia who attended the 1980 SITE.

From the point of view of the Federation American Baptist influence must be picked up in the ministry of Dr. Edwin A. Bell who, for 15 years until his retirement in 1960, served the cause of Baptists in Europe with devotion and distinction, particularly in relief and reconstruction work in postwar years.

He was succeeded by Dr. Gordon Lahrson who had previously served as professor of Homiletics at the Berkeley Divinity School, Berkeley, California. Dr. Lahrson devoted much of his time and energy to the strengthening of close ties with our Baptists in the socialist countries of Eastern Europe who, at that time, were severely restricted in any form of communication with their fellow Baptists in Europe.

On Dr. Lahrson's retirement American Baptist Churches' interest was expanded to the care of three representatives in Europe. Dr. Denton Lotz assumed responsibility for the continued strengthening of ties with Eastern Europe and also undertaking some teaching responsibility at the Baptist Theological Seminary in Rüschlikon. Dr. Lotz moved to Washington, D.C., to serve with the Baptist World Alliance in 1980 and has been succeeded by Dr. James Sprigg, who has the office at the Baptist Theological Seminary in Rüschlikon.

Dr. Maurice Entwistle, previously a missionary in the then Belgian Congo (Zaire), was asked to settle in Brussels, Belgium, and give help and encouragement to our small and hard-pressed Baptist people there and also in France. Dr. Entwistle continues his ministry to the blessing of all Baptists there.

The third area of International Ministries' interest was in Scandinavia where Rev. Rodger Harrison first came to work with Swedish Baptists. He was followed by Rev. James Jones who concentrated his work among Baptist young people and students in Uppsala. Later Rev. P. Reidar Lindland returned to Norway after working in Zaire and continued to work there until 1981.

Another important contribution of American Baptist Churches' International Ministries was the creation in Dr. Lahrson's ministry of the Baptist Lay Academy concept. In the early stages it was hoped that a building could be acquired in Sweden where a continuing ministry of lay persons' training could be developed. It was hoped particularly that this would enable lay persons from Baptist Unions in Eastern Europe to participate.

It did not prove possible to develop the building project, and eventually the program was carried through by a series of conferences in different centers in Eastern Europe. The program continues, and the latest conference was held in Poland in September of 1980.

The continuing financial annual contribution of American Baptist Churches' International Ministries to the general working budget of the European Baptist Federation has been one of the major factors in the developing work of the Federation. Burdened by the fact that most of its member unions were small in membership and also by the fact that two-thirds of Baptists in Europe live in the closed currency areas of Europe and therefore could make no contribution at all, the Federation was financially dependent to a great extent on help from outside of Europe. This help came and continues to come from American Baptist Churches' International Ministries.

The Baptist Theological Seminary, Rüschlikon: The Baptist Seminary, Rüschlikon, Zürich, Switzerland, to which reference has previously been made has played and continues to play a leading part in

the work of the Federation. The Baptist Seminary
is now jointly sponsored by the Southern Baptist
Convention Foreign Mission Board and the European
Baptist Federation.

It began as a rallying center for the fragmented Baptist life of Europe which was a result of
World War II. Gradually it developed as a Conference
Center bringing together Baptists from all over Europe for study, conference, and fellowship. Today
with its teaching program and as a Baptist Center
and Conference Center, the Baptist Seminary fulfills
a unique place in European Baptist life.

One of the particularly important areas of usefulness has been in relationship to Baptists in
Eastern Europe. As far as can be ascertained, there
is no other seminary in Europe of any denomination
which has students from U.S.S.R., Poland, Czechoslovakia, Hungary, Romania, and Yugoslavia in the student body as in the Baptist Seminary in Rüschlikon.

The value of the Baptist Seminary as a conference center can be illustrated by the recently developed SITE program. SITE stands for Summer Institute of Theological Education and is a one-month
period of theological education offered to pastors
and lay persons. Its primary aim is to provide these
theological education facilities for Baptists from
Eastern Europe. To these is presented, on completing
the course, a "mini-library" which the student takes
back and which forms the basis for continuing study.
The SITE program was initiated in Rüschlikon by Dr.
Denton Lotz and is a project of the European Baptist
Federation. From this can be seen the value of the
close working relationship between the Federation
and the Baptist Seminary.

Another most useful provision made by the
Southern Baptist Convention Foreign Mission Board to

Baptist life in Europe is the European Baptist Press Service. Although provided (financially and with personnel) and equipped by the Foreign Mission Board, it is under the direction of the European Baptist Federation. In September, 1976, the Press Service office moved from Paris to Zürich, Switzerland, where it is at present located in the Baptist Seminary building. It operates under the directorship of Mr. John Wilkes, a Southern Baptist Convention missionary.

Both American Baptist Churches and the Southern Baptist Convention were involved in the developing work of Baptist life in Europe through the Federation from the very beginning and continue to be.

The European Baptist Convention (English-speaking): However in more recent years another Baptist group has also joined to give help and encouragement in a very real way. The European Baptist Convention was welcomed as a member of the European Baptist Federation in 1970. The Convention is made up of a number of English-speaking Baptist churches in various areas of Western Europe. Its membership is mostly, but not entirely, made up of American service personnel stationed in Europe.

The Convention has gone from strength to strength, and in a most practical way has related closely to the national Baptist churches. So close has the relationship become that the Convention is a readily accepted working member of the Federation and makes a considerable contribution to the Federation's annual budget.

Missionaries from America: Although the Federation is made up of national Baption Unions in Europe, no table of influences which have taken part in the developing Baptist story can be complete without some reference being made to the missionary force

of American Baptist Churches' International Ministries and Southern Baptist Convention Foreign Mission
Board working within a number of Baptist Unions in
Europe. Certainly not only their influence has been
more apparent within the work and witness of the
national Baptist Unions with which they serve, but
also their influence in the wider life of the Federation has been appreciable.

It will be seen that while Baptists in Europe
have always demonstrated a degree of independence,
nevertheless without such supportive help as has
been demonstrated, it is doubtful if the Federation
could have begun its life; and even if it had been
born, it could not have been sustained.

The European Baptist Federation--A Service Unit

In 1974 a new Constitution for the Federation
was introduced which took into consideration the
trends and developments of former years. It was
particularly anxious to make clear that in no way
and at no time was there any possibility of the
Federation becoming a "Master Union" or of seeking
authority over Unions or churches.

The way of making this clear and accepted was
to emphasize the nature of the work of the Federation as a "service unit." In this was its strength
and in this it demonstrated its greatest usefulness.
It made clear in a number of ways that what could
not be imagined as a possibility by a small church
or group could, in fact, come to pass as a result
of joint action such as the Federation could provide.

Speaking in Behalf of Others: One of the earliest examples of this concerns the situation of our
Baptist people in Spain. In 1960 Baptists in Spain
were experiencing many difficulties through government discrimination against Protestant groups

throughout the country. At one time seven Baptist churches had been closed by government order and three pastors were imprisoned for noncompliance with discriminatory regulations.

At that time Dr. Erik Rudén, the Secretary/ Treasurer of the European Baptist Federation, began a series of interviews with government officials in Madrid and elsewhere. In these interviews he was able to answer questions and clear misunderstandings concerning Baptists and their position as Free Churches. Gradually the effect of this mediation was seen and in time the churches were opened and the pastors freed. Today the position in Spain is quite different and the churches of the Baptist Union are free and evangelizing with great effect.

Such action typied here has been repeated on numerous occasions and in a number of countries, and the ministry of "collective representation" has proved most effective. The value of "united action" becomes of increasing importance as communication becomes easier.

Establishing Communications Across New Barriers: The re-patterning of Europe after the Second World War presented Baptists with the unique problem of having two-thirds of their European brothers and sisters in the Communist countries of Europe. Consequently even more urgent than the building of new church buildings was the basic necessity of establishing communications. In the early days of that period it was unusual to receive a visa which granted permission to visit and preach in churches of Eastern Europe, and such visits were fraught with anxiety lest the visitor unwittingly should leave behind a legacy of harm.

In recent years there has been steady and continuous improvement in communication with all countries. The value of "united" or "collective" action becomes of increasing importance when circumstances arise, as they constantly do in Europe, which call for some form of intervention or representation on behalf of one group or another to secure for them justice and recognition of the rights of religious freedom. It may be, as illustrated, in the closing of a church; it may be in the more personal and painful terms of persecution and imprisonment; it may be in seeking permission to print hymnbooks or import Bibles. It should be made clear that not all the problems are caused by hostile government action but sometimes by the autocratic ecclesiasticism of national churches.

At such a time the voice that speaks and the action that is taken must have substantial backing; and for it to be effective, it must be known to be representative of many countries. Here it is that the European Baptist Federation can and does fulfill a most significant ministry.

In addition to this a number of similar instances of the effectiveness of joint representation can be listed and would, if space permitted, bear effective testimony to the worth of the European Baptist Federation to Baptist life in Europe.

Encourages Work With Special Groups: From the beginning the Federation has encouraged work on an international basis among women, men, and youth. Indeed, European Baptist Women's Union was in existence and operating successfully before the Federation came into existence. Working in conjunction with the Federation and also in membership with Baptist World Alliance Women's Union, it renders an outstanding service in uniting Baptist women throughout Europe in fellowship and service.

Likewise the Youth Committee through a variety

133

of conferences which have included youth leaders, teachers, students, etc., has introduced Baptist young people to each other across the diving barriers of language, culture, and history.

The Men's Committee has also served from the earliest days of the Federation's formation. It has served a most useful purpose but is not helped by the fact that in general European Baptist Unions do not put special emphasis on "Men's Work." Only two of the European Unions—United Kingdom and Denmark—have a department for "Men's Work" in their Union programs.

Establishes Committees for Special Functions: The above three "Committees" were a part of the earliest Federation program but it soon became evident that effective work could be done through other more specialized groups. The first to be formed was a Committee for "Bible Study and Membership Training" followed shortly afterwards by a Committee for "Radio and Television." This latter was largely brought about by the opening in the Baptist Seminary, Rüschlikon, of a well-equipped studio which could be used in giving practical experience to pastors who had the opportunity of doing radio work.

In the 1960s and early 70s Europe was faced with a vast population movement as immigrants from a number of countries sought security and hoped for prosperity in other areas of the Continent. This created a challenge to the European churches and Baptists were quickly involved in seeking ways and means of playing their part. A "Migration Committee" was formed as part of the work of the Federation. Over a period conferences for those most closely involved in the problems and opportunities of the church/immigrant relationships were organized with a number of resultant programs coming into effect. Eventually the whole vast problem became too much for any one group or denomination and more ecumenically cooperative programs took the place of most of the work of the Immigration Committee.

The increasing interest in and emphasis on Evangelism and Church Growth during the 1970s brought about the formation of the "Evangelism and Education" Committee. In all member Unions of the Federation the challenge of Christian witness was being faced, but amidst such a variety of local and national conditions no one pattern or program was applicable or even practical.

Here again the value of joint action rather than individual national action became clear. The Evangelism and Education Committee brought representatives from all areas of Europe together in conferences, and here problems were faced in mutual concern and experiences in programs and projects of outreach were shared. In addition Baptist personnel experienced in these fields of Christian witness were brought in from other parts of the world. Such has been the effectiveness of these "Evangelism and Education" conferences that they are now held annually at the Baptist Seminary in Rüschlikon.

An area in which the European Baptist Federation has been especially effective as a "service unit" is in "Relief and Development" work. A whole separate article could usefully be written on the various projects undertaken by the concerted action of Baptist people. However, many of these have been undertaken in joint action with the Baptist World Alliance Relief Committee, as for instance the building of new churches in Eastern Europe such as in Warsaw, Poland; Cheb, Czechoslovakia; Arad, Romania; in Novi Sad, Yugoslavia; and in Hungary, and in other countries. Perhaps one of the most dramatic acts of united concern was in response to the devasting earthquake in Italy in December, 1980.

Unity in Diversity

Earlier reference has been made to the need for some unifying organization to exist in an area of Baptist life where so much difference and diversity exists.

It seems valuable, therefore, to enlarge in detail on an area in Europe where Baptist life is lived in unusual circumstances and that is in the "Socialist" countries of Eastern Europe. In each Communist country of Europe, except Albania, there are Baptist churches with an organized Baptist Union or Convention. All of these began in the days before the 1917 Revolution, survived the Nazi occupation, and are more than surviving under the regime of atheistic humanism.

In 1955 it could be written: "The European Baptist Federation cannot at present be truly representative of all European Baptist churches, for many of them are cut off from any effective personal communication from their fellow Christians in the West." In recent years, however, there has been a general improvement in the situation.

All the Unions in Eastern Europe are now members of the European Baptist Federation and the Baptist World Alliance, and communication with them is improving. From time to time restrictions on travel, both into and out of these countries, have caused serious problems and disappointments.

On the other hand, officers of the Baptist World Alliance and the European Baptist Federation have, in recent years, made repeated visits to all the Eastern European Baptist Unions. A growing sense of unity and fellowship exists. It has been possible for the European Baptist Federation to elect a president from the U.S.S.R.--the Rev. Michael Zhidkov of

Moscow. Baptist representatives from Poland, Czechoslovakia, Yugoslavia, and the U.S.S.R. have in turn served effectively on the Federation Executive Committee.

Suffering as a Sect: In writing of the situation of the Christian church in socialist countries, and of Baptists in particular, it is necessary to understand something of the background and of the pressures which produce the modern situation.

Perhaps the first thing of importance is not the restrictions of the law on Christian organizations. Rather it is that in each of these countries there has been a long history of religion and a strong state church which dominated the religious life of the country. One of the effects of this domination was seen in the attitude towards other branches of the Christian faith.

So much has been written about the difficulties of the Christian church under Communist Marxism that we forget that minority groups--such as Baptists-- had a very hard time under previous regimes. The Orthodox Church in Russia, Romania, and Bulgaria regarded Baptists as a "sect" and, indeed, in theological terms still does. Where the voice of the strong national church is still listened to, the pressure from these bodies is more painful than the legal restrictions imposed by the state, which are often a reflection of this ecclesiastical pressure.

For instance, it is a precept of the Orthodox Church that all who leave "the fold" and become members of another communion are "victims of sheep stealing" or proselytizing. Proselytizing is forbidden by statute. But Baptists believe in the importance of personal faith through conversion and go out to make converts. Their success marks them as criminals and the law takes its effect upon them. Although this law is imposed by government, it is created by historic ecclesiastic tradition.

Improved Conditions: But the coming of Communism has improved the situation of Baptists and other minority groups in some places. In Poland, before the war, the Roman Catholic Church, which held similar views of proselytism, had complete control of the country. Although Polish Baptists then were stronger numerically than today, their life was hard; for they were regarded as a sect and treated as such.

Here a rule of socialist law that "all religions should be regarded as equal" has been applied to the great benefit of Baptists and other minority groups.

In the U.S.S.R. a similar situation exists. Under the Czars before the 1917 Communist revolution, Baptists suffered double opposition from the state and the Orthodox Church, which was then the state church. Many Baptist leaders were imprisoned or exiled and many "prayer houses" were closed or burned. Some older Baptists claim that they have greater freedom today than under the old regime.

In other areas of Europe, chiefly in Romania and Bulgaria, only lip service is paid to the law that all religions are equal. It is observed with little enthusiasm or not at all. So minority groups there continue to suffer opposition and persecution.

This criticism needs some qualification. While we are naturally concerned with the conditions under which our own people have to live and worship, we must not forget that these strong national churches are bulwarks against the atheism and materialism of state doctrine.

<u>What Kind of Freedom?</u> Keeping in mind the re-
ligious background, we ask what are the conditions
under which a church is permitted to exist in a
country whose government holds an atheistic ideology.

The situation of the church in the Soviet Union
arouses much interest and concern. It has been said
that if the Soviet Union would abide by its own laws,
much of the discrimination would disappear. This,
at best, is only partly true. For although some
guarantees of the individual's rights are contained
in the Soviet constitution—its supreme law—these
rights can, in practice, be negated by the application of the penal code. In no area is this more
damaging to the rights of the individual than in his
religious life.

The Soviet law declares church and state to be
separated. It further makes it clear that discrimination against the individual for reasons of his religious adherence is a punishable offense. These
originally were Leninist principles.

The first decree of the Soviet state on religion, in the formulation of which Lenin himself had
considerable say, proclaimed that it was illegal "to
restrain or limit freedom of conscience" and that
"every citizen may profess any religion or none at
all." This was reflected in the first constitution
(July 1918) which stated that "the right to religious
and anti-religious propaganda is recognized for all
citizens."

This was amended in May, 1929, to exclude the
"right to religious propaganda." The present Article 124 of the constitution reads even more severely
with "the freedom to hold religious services" as
the believers' sole right. Here a significant distinction must be noted. "Freedom to hold religious

services"--not the right to religious propaganda. This invidious distinction permits the state full rights of anti-religious propaganda, while the church has no such right.

Church Services Restricted: Further, the interpretation of "holding religious services" is entirely in the hands of the state. In practice it reduces all Christian activity to that which can be exercised within a building set aside for religious purposes.

Such a building has to be state registered, and to hold services in any other place offends the law and leaves the offenders open to severe penal action. (The issue of registered buildings is referred to later.) For worship anywhere else permission must be sought at least two weeks in advance, and there is no certainty this will be granted.

This affects Baptists in a particular way. Some extremist groups, whose statements are sometimes based on partial truths, assert that there can be no outside baptisms in the U.S.S.R. or in any other Communist country. Now many of our rural Baptist churches (registered buildings) are not equipped with baptistries. They must therefore use whatever means they can, and this often means a nearby river or stream. Permission for this kind of baptism must be sought well in advance. But this cannot in any way be interpreted as "no outside baptisms." For while permission is sometimes denied and is often delayed, there are many well known occasions where these services have been permitted.

Other restrictions include the limiting of the clergy's activities to their own areas, an absolute ban on all relief work, no discussion groups, and no Sunday school or youth work.

Within the registered building there is freedom

to preach and to baptize, although each candidate's name must be submitted to the Office of the Department of Religion and Cult. (In all my visits to churches in the U.S.S.R. I have never been asked to submit a manuscript before preaching nor have I been warned what to say or not to say, save that I have been exhorted to "preach the gospel of our Lord Jesus Christ.")

Dissident Groups: "The registered building" is one of the basic reasons for the emergence of "dissident groups" in the U.S.S.R. These groups are named together under the "Initisiativniki" and comprise those who came out of the official Baptist Union, called the All Union Council of Evangelical Christians-Baptists, and later formed an unofficial group called The Council of Churches of the Evangelical Christians and Baptists.

This group originally went into schism from the All Union Council not for any theological or doctrinal reason, but because certain leaders wanted to take extreme measures in order to secure a more definite separation between church and state.

The All Union Council of Evangelical Christians-Baptists declared their position by accepting the scriptural injunction of Romans 13* as being binding upon upon their churches and accepting such limitations as are imposed, providing they are free to preach the gospel of the Lord Jesus Christ, make converts, and to baptize.

In separating from the All Union Council of Evangelical Christians-Baptists, the "reform groups"

---

*Romans 13:1 "Let every person be subject to the governing authorities."

immediately brought themselves outside of the law in that they could not secure registered places of worship. Whenever and wherever they met it had to be in secret. This transgressed the law. The law against them has been imposed with severity, and sad and utterly regrettable suffering has been the result.

The All Union Council of Evangelical Christians-Baptists, deeply conscious of the problems of their separated brethren, has made repeated attempts to bring about reconciliation and restore the sadly divided church. Many, both pastors and members, who formerly were within the dissident groups, have returned to the All Union Council and have been gladly and warmly received back. It is estimated that between five and eight thousand remain in the separated groups.

Restrictions occur in other ways and strict state control of religious activity in such areas as printing of Bibles and religious literature, limitation on theological training, and possibilities of international Christian fellowship are hard to bear.

How Can They Stand It? These numerous restrictions imposed upon the church would seem to people in the Western world seriously to curtail the Christian program and to restrict personal religious freedom. How can Christian people accept these restructions and live under them?

The answer to this has been put quite graphically by one of our leaders from Eastern Europe who said very simply, "While we have the freedom to preach the gospel and to make converts and baptize them, we are happy; and we are prepared to accept the restrictions. While the door is open wide enough for us to do this, we will not push it in case it should come back in our faces and what we have should be lost."

There is no doubt that they are free to preach the gospel. Their general position seems to be summarized in the statement that they are happy to accept socialist ideology in politics but to stand against the doctrine of atheism.

Let it be understood that socialism has brought material blessings to large numbers of people in Eastern Europe who, before the 1917 revolution, lived in want and under severe restriction and hardship. It is therefore perhaps not surprising that they are happy to stay in their country as good patriots but would seek to do everything in their power to be true to their Christian faith and their Lord and Savior.

Conclusion

This brief outline of the history and work of the European Baptist Federation is only the "bare bones" of a story which indicates an exciting development in Baptist interrelationship.

Realizing as we are constantly made to do the reckless individualism and unhappy isolationism of some of our Baptist brethren, it might be considered as miraculous that such a degree of cooperation has been achieved. As hard as this is to achieve, the important thing is that it is increasing and this practical tribute is made of the work of the Federation.

The Federation will never become a "governing" body among European Baptists because it has no ambition whatever in that direction. It will develop and increase in its usefulness as a "Service Unit," and its areas of work will undoubtedly be expanded as more and more doors of opportunity are opened in every part of Europe.

CHAPTER 5

1. Appendix I. Minutes of a meeting called to form the European Baptist Federation, October 20 and 21, 1950.
2. Appendix II. First Constitution of European Baptist Federation and minutes of the inaugural meeting of October 20-21, 1950.
3. Now "International Ministries of the American Baptist Churches."
4. Baptist work in Finland is divided into two Unions. The Finnish-speaking Finnish Baptist Union and the Swedish-speaking Finnish Baptist Union. The separation is caused by the fact that Finnish is an extremely difficult language to learn.
5. Appendix III. List of European Baptist Federation Secretary/Treasurers.

Baptisms in Riga, Latvia, 1978, give evidence of effective evangelism in a communist country. Other socialist countries also report church growth.

BAPTISTS IN EUROPE--1980

COUNTRY	POPULATION	CHURCHES	MEMBERS
Austria	7,500,000	9	691
Belgium	9,860,000	8	512
Bulgaria	9,000,000	10	650
Czechoslovakia	15,360,000	28	3,978
Denmark	5,140,000	41	6,362
Europe--European			
Baptist Convention		40	3,847
(English Language)			
Finland	4,770,000		
Finnish speaking		10	771
Swedish speaking		24	1,712
France	53,680,000	28	2,997
Germany			
Democratic Republic	16,720,000	215	21,193
Federal Republic	61,350,000	356	68,012
Hungary	10,720,000	200	12,000
Italy	57,100,000	80	4,200
Netherlands	14,125,000	81	11,951
Norway	4,085,000	64	6,299
Poland	35,450,000	55	2,539
Portugal	9,940,000	52	2,800
Romania	22,300,000	662	160,000
Spain	37,575,000	61	4,800
Sweden	8,300,000	422	21,651
Switzerland	6,345,000	15	1,425
U.S.S.R.	265,750,000	5,000	545,000
United Kingdom	55,800,000		
Great Britain &			
Ireland		2,091	174,578
Scotland		157	14,429
Yugoslavia	22,310,000	61	3,484
	733,180,000	9,770	1,075,881

EUROPE in 1970

☐ U.S.S.R. in 1938
▨ Acquired by U.S.S.R. 1939~1945
▧ Soviet Satellites
▨ Communist, but not a Satellite
▢ North Atlantic Treaty Organization ★

Arctic Ocean

NORWAY
SWEDEN
FINLAND

Atlantic Ocean

GREAT BRITAIN
IRELAND

ESTONIA
LATVIA
LITHUANIA

UNION of
SOVIET SOCIALIST REPUBLIC

• Moscow

DENMARK
NETHER-LANDS
London
BELGIUM
Paris
LUXEMBURG
FRANCE
GERMANY
• Bonn
FEDERAL
REPUBLIC
SWITZER-LAND

POLISH ADMIN.
GER. DEM. REPUB.
Berlin
Danzig
POLAND
CZECHOSLOVAKIA
Vienna
AUSTRIA
HUNGARY
ROUMANIA

Boundary of
U.S.S.R. in 1938

SPAIN
• Madrid
PORTUGAL

ITALY
Rome

YUGOSLAVIA
BULGARIA

Black Sea

TURKEY

Mediterranean

GREECE
ALBANIA

Sea

★ Plus Canada, Iceland, and the United States.

146

CHAPTER 6

MAGNIFICENT IN WITNESS AND SERVICE TODAY

SCANDINAVIA

Denmark, Norway, Sweden, Finland
Knud Wumpelmann

The state church tradition is very strong in
Scandinavia. It has now played an important role
for one thousand years. Since the Reformation 450
years ago, the Lutheran Church has been the one
dominating church in Scandinavia. Even today more
than 90 percent of the population of these countries
are said to be Lutherans. Out of a total Scandinavian population of 22,285,000 people, only 37,795
are baptized members of the Baptist churches. In
addition the number of participants in children's
and youth work is about the same as the number of
church members. Therefore the combined figures for
church membership and youth participation amounts to
only three-tenths of 1 percent of the population.

Although the Baptist movement is the oldest
Free Church movement and the Baptist church in part
of Scandinavia still is the strongest Free Church,
it certainly has remained a small minority group
within each of these countries.[1]

A number of reasons for this could be mentioned.

Let it be enough here to remember the fact that when Baptists—after centuries of persecution, suppression, and discrimination in Europe—came to America and there found a country where all denominations had to work under equal conditions, the Baptist movement certainly grew stronger.

The following question, however, has to be asked: "Is such a small minority church as the Baptist church in Scandinavia of any importance at all?" To some persons successful church-growth statistics seem to be the only thing that really matters. But church-growth rates, greatly important as they certainly are, should not be seen as the only way in which the witness and service of a church can be measured.

It is encouraging to see the following evaluation from outside of Free Church influence in Scandinavia. Dr. P. G. Lindhardt, the well-known Lutheran professor of church history, says in his book on the history of the Scandinavian church: "The influence of most of the Free Churches goes beyond that which would be expected, the membership figures taken into consideration."[2] This influence has been and is still being felt within the church life of these countries and as part of the church's service to the world.

Baptists in a State Church Situation

The Baptist role in a state church situation is to serve as a necessary supplement and even corrective of what can be offered by a state church to the people. The Baptist church must, in order to fulfill its task in a state church country, be a kind of a catalyst.

The Baptist way of emphasizing the need for a personal decision for Christ by combining conversion

148

with baptism and the democratic church organization of a Baptist church, based as it is on the understanding of the responsibility of ordinary church members for the activities and the finances of the church, are some of the most important issues to be mentioned in this connection.

As pointed out by Professor Karl Barth, a state church can only exist on the basis of infant baptism, and infant baptism as practiced in a state church is probably the most severe handicap of the state church system. Indiscriminate infant baptism, which to so many people only functions as a name-giving rite with no deeper religious meaning at all and with no Christian background in the home in which the child is to grow up, will work more like an effective serum against Christianity than as a good beginning of a Christian life as it certainly was intended to be. The result is seen in a very low church attendance--in Copenhagen, for example, only about 1 percent of the population are in church on an ordinary Sunday. Furthermore it is difficult to defend infant baptism as the very entrance of the individual into the body of Christ and at the same time to be a true member of his church. The Baptist corrective is here very much needed.

During the last 10 to 20 years a totally new situation has occurred in the old Lutheran churches of Scandinavia--especially in the big cities. For example, in Copenhagen no more than two-thirds of the babies are being baptized (in some parishes it is even less than 50 percent). Although parents usually are not leaving the church, they want their children to decide for themselves in due time if they want to become members of the church. This new situation is of course a challenge to the Baptists as well as to the Lutherans.

Another handicap of the state church system is

that it may function with a minimum of personal interest on the part of its constituency, while the Baptist church is very dependent not only on the financial support of its members but also on their participation in the life and work of the church.

The pastor in a state church may say—as one of them, serving a church with a very low attendance, did in a newspaper interview—"The church is like a street car—it runs on schedule whether or not there are passengers who want to use it." The church building, the pastor, the organist, the choir, etc., are all paid for whether or not the congregation cares. To carry responsibilities should, however, be one of the real blessings of belonging to a church fellowship. In a Free Church this is indispensable. Here an active congregation is a "must." This is probably one of the main reasons why new initiatives in church life often come from the Free Churches.

In many places it was in the Free Churches that the Sunday school work began and grew strong. Among Scandinavian Baptists, the scout work and similar organizations for children and youth have been closely related to the church work, and a good part of the new members came into the church through these organizations. For a number of years two-thirds of the Baptist scouts in Denmark have come from non-Baptist homes, and one-third of the scouts who became members of the church came from non-Baptist homes. The women's work has also been an important activity within the Baptist churches. In Sweden 6,000 women out of a total church membership of 21,651 belong to the Baptist Women's Union, and the same is true about the temperance movement which has been especially strong within the Free Churches. And in the Scandinavian Baptist churches the free-will offerings to local and cooperative missions came to an average of approximately $300 per member in 1979.

The Training of Leadership

One of the advantages of a state church is the high academic standard of its professional leaders. One of its disadvantages is, however, that the pastors are trained more in theory than in practice. This situation is another challenge to the Baptist Unions in Scandinavia.

Scandinavian Baptist seminaries are rather small--from about 60 students at different levels at the Swedish Bethel Seminary in Stockholm and 15 at the seminary in Oslo down to normally 6 to 8 theological students at the seminary at Töllöse in Denmark. The Finnish Baptists are sending their students either to Bethel Seminary in Stockholm or to the cooperative Baptist Theological Seminary at Rüschlikon, Switzerland.

The number of students corresponds to the number of churches in the five Unions. In Sweden there are 414 churches with an average membership of 51 persons, in Norway 64 churches with an average of 98 members, in Denmark 41 churches with an average of 156 members, and in the Swedish-speaking Finnish Baptist mission 24 churches with an average of 71 members. The Finnish Baptist Union has 10 churches with an average of 77 members.

The handicaps of a small seminary are to a certain extent balanced by the advantages of working together in small groups, of having a more flexible curriculum, and of being able to combine closely the practical and the theoretical education through the whole period of the study. In order to be able to take advantage of the theological education at the state universities before or after the studies at the Baptist seminaries, part of the curriculum in the seminaries is, where possible, planned so that credit can be given for these studies.

With a strong emphasis in the seminaries on training the students to be pastors, well-equipped to serve a Free Church with all its many activities, the need exists for supplementary theological education. A good number of Baptist pastors seek such education--often after some years of practical service in a church--at the Baptist Seminary at Rüschlikon, at state universities, or at a theological seminary in the U.S.A. The help received from the American Baptist Churches in the U.S.A. to arrange for such studies has been greatly appreciated. American Baptists--in later years in cooperation with Southern Baptists--have greatly supported the building of national theological seminaries in Scandinavia; thus they have in a most strategic way helped the Scandinavian Baptist Unions to serve and to witness.

The training of the lay people in the churches is just as important as the education of pastors. Within this area much help has been received through this century from American Baptists. The People's High School is a special Scandinavian feature. Its origin goes back to the middle of the nineteenth century at the time in Denmark when the absolute monarch was to be taken over by a democratic government. N.F.S. Grundtvig, the great hymn writer and church leader, saw that this important change needed a spiritual preparedness of the people if it should succeed. Therefore he took the initiative to start the People's High School--a movement inviting men and women from 18 years and up to come together to get to know better the history, the literature, and song treasures of the people as well as their Christian beliefs, responsibilities, and challenges in a new situation. The courses should last from six to nine months. There should be no exams and no diplomas, but great emphasis was to be laid upon fellowship through singing, discussion, and living together.

This movement grew strong within the state church during the later part of the nineteenth century. In 1884 it was Professor N. P. Jensen from Morgan Park, Illinois, who encouraged the annual conference of the Danish Baptists to found the first People's High School outside the Lutheran Church. In 1891 the school was started by a school teacher, N. K. Kristoffersen. It has during the years given a high percentage of the young Baptists a strong feeling of belonging to a wider Baptist fellowship, practical help to serve better as leaders in their own churches, and a wider understanding of their responsibilities as Christian citizens. The People's High School idea spread to all the other Scandinavian countries where it was adapted to the different needs in each place. Very much needed financial help for some of these school projects has come from American Baptists.

When the Lay Academy idea spread in Germany and other parts of Europe after World War II, Dr. Gordon Lahrson, field representative in Europe for the American Baptist Foreign Mission Society, took the initiative to help Baptists in northern Europe to adapt this idea to their situation. The result was that American Baptists offered to the Scandinavian Baptists a fund of $25,000 taken from the World Mission Campaign resources to be used for such a project. As a result, since 1970 a Lay Conference has been arranged every year (sometimes for Scandinavians only); often for northern and eastern Europeans.

Some of the conferences have been arranged for professional groups such as medical doctors, nurses, pastors, Christian journalists, social workers, and workers with elderly people (together with representatives of this age group). Recently another $25,000 has been granted to the Lay Academy Fund to make it possible to invite eastern Europeans to participate regularly in the conferences. Three of

the conferences have been held in eastern Europe.
The personal contacts between Baptists from the east
and from the north have been very inspiring and encouraging and perhaps more important than many peace
talks for the furtherance of better understanding
between the two blocks of nations within Europe.

Baptists Serving the World

There are 125 Scandinavian Baptist missionaries
serving in Zaire, Tanzania, Rwanda, Burundi, India,
Japan, Thailand, and Brazil. This means that there
is one active missionary in international ministries
for every 300 church members at home. Finland's
Swedish-speaking Baptists have one missionary for
every 170 members.

The Missionary Society of the Swedish Baptists
which was organized in 1889 is the oldest. In 1891
it entered the field in China, and the following
year missionaries were sent to the Belgian Congo.
Norwegian Baptists started work in the northern part
of the Republic of Congo in 1915. Danish Baptists
began in 1928 in Burundi as the only Protestant mission in that country at the time. The independent
African churches with which Norwegian and Danish
Baptists are cooperating today have more than three
times as many members as their Scandinavian "mother"
churches. Six years ago the Swedish Baptist Union
extended its work to include Thailand as the third
Asian country in which Swedish Baptist missionaries
are working. Their main work is, however, still
being done in Zaire. Finnish missionaries have
through the years been highly appreciated co-workers
in other Scandinavian international ministries.

Before organizing their own missionary societies, Scandinavian Baptists participated in the work
of the American Baptist Foreign Mission Society to
which Danish Baptists were sending all their foreign

154

mission offerings from 1877 to 1919. Today American and Scandinavian missionaries are working together as partners in multilateral mission work in a number of places.

Strong financial support is received from SIDA (Swedish International Development Assistance). Also the Norwegian state gives substantial financial help to foreign mission work, but Finnish and Danish government aid (only to a very limited extent) has been given to the development work of foreign mission organizations.

In Norway near the North Cape a home for deep-sea fishermen was established in 1921 and rebuilt after World War II. In 1951 a fishing boat was purchased with the help of Baptists in the U.S.A. to function as a sailing mission station, equipped with loudspeaker and the like, to serve the district north of the Arctic Circle. In 1947 on Norwegian initiative the Scandinavian Baptists sent their first seamen's missionary, Rev. Thorbjörn Olsen, to the West Coast of the U.S.A. to serve among Scandinavian seamen. During the years great support has been received from American Baptist churches in the area for the Scandinavian Seamen's Mission in San Francisco.

The Swedish Baptists have a special organization for social mission. Its work in Sweden includes: activities among guest [migrant and immigrant] workers of which there are about 800,000 in Sweden, help to different groups of handicapped persons, and work among pensioners. Outside Sweden the social mission is responsible for relief work and development aid in a number of countries. Scandinavian Baptists are also supporting the relief work of the Baptist World Alliance and the European Baptist Federation as well as the ecumenical national relief organizations. Two Swedish pastors are serving part-time as hospital chaplains and one as a student pastor.

Baptists in Ecumenical Cooperation

Julius Köbner, whose influence among the earliest Scandinavian Baptists was of great importance (as we have seen earlier in this book) was very alliance-minded. "All believers in the whole world are my dear brothers in Christ," he said, "whether they are Catholics, Lutherans, Reformed...whether they are pastors or lay people. With all of them I want to be one on earth as some day we shall be one in Heaven."[3]

In 1851 Köbner together with Oncken and Lehmann attended the great Evangelical Alliance Congress in London. An appeal from this meeting to found an Evangelical Alliance in Germany was immediately signed by the three Baptist leaders from Hamburg, but the Lutherans in Germany were not ready to establish such fellowship. This historical background is typical also for the later relationship between the Scandinavian Baptists and the ecumenical movement.

In parts of Scandinavia it took a long time before Baptists and other Free Churches were invited to participate in organizations which on the international level were basically ecumenical--the Bible Society, the Missionary Council, the Evangelical Alliance, and others--while Baptists themselves usually were eager to work for Christian unity.

Ecumenical cooperation on the local level has especially developed in Sweden during later years due to two main circumstances: (1) In a number of small villages some of the Free Churches came together under different organizational setups in order to survive, because most of the young people in these places move to larger cities to find education and work, causing a constant decline in membership in these churches. (2) In many of the new suburban districts which have been built during more recent years around the big cities in Sweden, the city authorities would offer one lot for a Lutheran Church and one for a Free Church, leaving it up to the Free Churches to decide among themselves who should have the opportunity to build this church. Also in this situation a close cooperation between the Free Churches involved was necessary, making "open" or "associated" membership a natural solution in most cases.

As a practical need and a natural consequence following the cooperation on the local level, serious attempts were made in the '70s to unite the old Free Churches into one--The Swedish Free Church--but this plan had finally to be given up.

In Sweden the influence of the Free Churches is much stronger than in any other of the Scandinavian countries. One of the main reasons for this is seen in the fact that when at the beginning of the nineteenth century a spiritual revival came to Scandinavia in the form of a strong lay people's movement, this revival was not at all accepted by the Swedish Lutheran Church; thus this stream of new life found its way almost totally through the Free Churches, while in Norway and Denmark the Lutheran Church opened up to a much greater degree for this revival.

The Free Church Council plays an important role in Sweden. For instance, the views of this council are usually being sought in legislation related to church life and to ethical questions. The Study Union of the Free Churches--an organization related to the Free Church Council--publishes a good number of study books every year. In 1979, 600 study circles were organized by this Union within the Baptist churches--one-half of them working with song and music, and the second half working with Bible and Christian life subjects.

The relationship between state and church has been critically evaluated on government level in Sweden and in Norway during recent years. The Swedish Free Church Council has, of course, been much involved in this work. In Norway a committee of 12 was appointed in 1970. In Oslo Jens Öen, one of the committee members, was the principal of the Baptist People's High School. Detailed proposals for new legislation separating state and church more from one another in order to give the Lutheran Church more freedom and responsibility has been presented in both countries. So far it has, however, not been possible to make any greater changes in the state church relationship, although Sweden came very close to a far-reaching reform.

At the beginning of the '60s the Ecumenical Council in Denmark appointed a study commission to discuss the different aspects of baptism. The commission was composed of three Lutherans, two Roman Catholics, two Baptists, and one Methodist. Some very interesting theses came out of this study work with unexpected strong support for some of the main Baptist viewpoints--especially on the close relationship between faith and baptism. Indiscriminate baptism of infants was, therefore, condemned; but at the same time Baptists were asked to rethink their total refusal of infant baptism and to consider the possibility of "open membership" which at that time had not yet been practiced among Danish Baptists. Even the official Catholic Weekly supported the findings of the commission. A fruitful discussion was started in all the churches involved, and this is still going on.

The ecumenical climate has, certainly, turned a little more mild during the last two decades, but much has still to be done. Scandinavian Baptists are now participating in almost all ecumenical organizations; however, only the Danish Baptist Union is a member of the World Council of Churches. The charismatic movement has in a different way--perhaps more on the grass-roots level--brought Christians from different denominations together. Also of importance has been some large, national ecumenical conferences modeled after the German "Kirchentag" pattern.

Do Scandinavian Baptists Have a Future?

Scandinavian Baptists have experienced a decline in membership. In the '30s the Örebro Mission was separated from the Swedish Baptist Union. Before the split there were 68,500 members in the Baptist churches. Now the membership of the two together has fallen to a total of about 40,000. In Denmark and Norway the decline began after World War II, and the membership fallen from 10 to 20 percent. In Sweden and Denmark surveys made by specialists in sociology of religion concerning the expected development during the coming years are not encouraging at all.

Is it possible under such circumstances to believe in a "magnificent future" for Scandinavian Baptists?

Scandinavian Baptists are convinced that, in the days to come, there will be also the need for a democratic minority church with emphasis upon personal faith in Christ and on Christian education. They know their own weaknesses quite well, but at the same time they want to be at the disposal of the Lord of mission--ready to be used by him in the way he wants and in his time. They see some signs of hope in a new attitude among the young people, in growing concern in the churches for the world around them, and in a wakening spiritual hunger in the people which seems to follow the years of constant material progress in Scandinavian welfare countries since World War II.

---

1. By Free Church is meant a church free in its relation to the state.
2. P. G. Lindhardt, Den Nordiske Kirkes Historie (Copenhagen, 1945), p. 223.
3. Arne Jensen, Julius Köbner (Copenhagen, 1947), pp. 80-81.

Tent evangelism has proved to be effective in Finland. The Finnish Baptist Union tent can accommodate 500 persons.

WESTERN EUROPE

France, Belgium, The Netherlands
Maurice S. Entwistle*

West Germany, Austria, Switzerland
Denton Lotz

Religious expression no longer occupies the central place it once had in society. Adherence to a church today is more a function of personal commitment than a civic function, regardless of the church. As a result, the actual number of communicant or practicing members is much smaller than those who consider themselves within the influence of a particular form of Christianity. This has produced in some circles a tendency to refer to these lands where state churches once held absolute power as post-Christian societies, since so few citizens actually determine their behavior in terms of the Christian faith.

One of the by-products of this phenomenon is the reduced impact in these areas of one of the Baptist distinctives, the emphasis on "freedom of conscience." In many areas of Europe today, people simply accept their right to adopt their own beliefs

---

*Editor's Note: All of the textual material, with the exception of that which describes Baptist work in West Germany, Austria, and Switzerland, has been excerpted from a ninety-page manuscript written by Maurice S. Entwistle especially for this book. It is with regret that we cannot present in full the carefully written historical, social, political, economic, and religious background material written for France, Belgium, and The Netherlands.

as a "given" in modern society and fail to realize how long and hard the struggle has been to make this God-given right a reality. So Baptists are not perceived today in this part of Europe as champions of unrecognized religious and personal liberties, as they were in the past century. As a result, Baptist growth has not been spectacular in the twentieth century as in past centuries. And in some areas it has been difficult for Baptists—along with other Christian churches—to even maintain their number as congregations were emptied by migration to the anonymity of urban areas, declared irrelevant or attacked by secular philosophies of life, and disrupted by war and economic upheaval in this past century.

Baptist Church Life in Western Europe

(FRANCE)

As mentioned earlier in this book, French Baptists first began to appear in France in 1810. In 1832 the Baptist Missionary Union sent John Casmir Rostan, a French immigrant, back to his native land as a missionary pastor. Unfortunately, he was stricken while ministering to the sick in Paris during a cholera epidemic and died a little over a year after his return. Baptist work, nevertheless, went on.

In 1835 the first Baptist church was organized in Paris. By 1845 there were seven churches. By 1945 there were 21 churches with 1,030 members. Twenty-five years later there were 44 churches with 2,468 members in 1970. In 1980 there were 67 churches with 2,997 members. In the past decade French Baptists grew by over 20 percent.

These figures are impressive when placed in the overall context that both Protestants and Roman

Catholics have barely held their own in the same ten-year period. Furthermore, the figures hide the fact that much of this growth has taken place in newly established churches.

Between 1970 and 1980 French Baptist support of their home mission outreach has tripled, going from about $12,000 a year to over $38,000. During that same period French Baptists began 23 new churches. In 1970 the churches under the home mission program contributed $67,570 toward their own support and the national program. In 1979 the new churches were contributing $322,000 for their own life and that of the French Baptist Federation. In other words, growth was a little over 20 percent in the past decade; the number of congregations increased by over 50 percent, and giving more than quadrupled.

In 1970 French Baptists entered their new study center, "Les CEDRES," at Massy, one of the Paris suburbs. French Baptists are too small to have their own university or seminary, but they had long dreamed of an orientation center for their people. It was made possible by the joint contributions of French Baptists, Southern Baptists, and American Baptists. The Center at Massy has accommodations for about forty single residents. So the Center offers accommodations to a large number of young adults who work or are in training in the Paris area, sponsors three small schools, and provides space for printing, publishing, studio recording, and a new church.

At Massy the "Ecole Pastorale" usually has about a half dozen candidates for the Baptist ministry who have completed their theological studies elsewhere and are doing a two-year orientation program of quarterly seminars on Baptist church life and work. The second year seminars are also used by pastors in service for continuing education. The

"Centre de Formation Biblique et Pratique" offers a year of residential study to about a dozen people a year who want to explore the implications of their faith in relation to church membership and their work. And the "Ecole de Langues" provides a year of French language study for about a dozen missionaries who have been appointed by various European churches for work in the developing nations which use French.

The Publishing Division at the Center prints about 50,000 copies a month of a small paper which is used by Baptists and several other Protestant churches for evangelization and news about church life. Each quarter it also publishes about 5,000 copies of a new paperback on a subject of interest for Christians. And it also provides individual churches with material they need for evangelistic campaigns or missions.

The Center's Recording Studio prepares a weekly thirty-minute recording for French Baptist outreach by radio, and also provides program material for radio ministries in Africa, Madagascar, and the Caribbean for various missions. In addition, the Studio offers the opportunity for young French Christians to record their witness through modern and traditional music forms for cassette distribution. This latter ministry has been made available to other Christian communions and is widely appreciated.

And finally, the Center was established in Massy to provide an opportunity for beginning a new church in this area. Outreach was begun about five years ago, and a worshiping community now meets regularly in the chapel area. This is characteristic of French Baptists who have a vision and a burden to reach their fellow citizens for Christ.

The use French Baptists make of their Center at

Les CEDRES, Massy, France, provided French Baptists with facilities for residential study, publishing, conferences, and institutes.

A coffee house over a canal in The Netherlands.

Massy is typical of their overall ministry. They emphasize the ministry of the local church for Jesus Christ. But this is seen as a cooperative endeavor where the churches actively support one another to overcome their problems and to increase the effectiveness of their witness. They have a strong identity as Baptists, but they see the Body of Christ, his church, as larger than their immediate fellowship. So they also support and share in the ministry of cooperative Christianity. Their publications are used by a number of other churches; their expertise on radio and cassette recording is used by both churches in France and by missions overseas, and they have made time available on the local and national level to back joint efforts by French churches concerning social issues and evangelistic outreach.

American Baptists have a long tradition of sharing the burden with their French brethren. One of the first churches we helped them build is on the Left Bank at 48 Rue de Lille in Paris. It was built in 1873 primarily for American residents, but a French congregation, established in 1854, was invited to share the use of the building from the outset. Some of the members of this French congregation traced their conversion back to the ministry of John Casmir Rostan.

Events later led the French to form two other congregations, one in 1894 on the same side of the river, and in 1924 in another part of the city. The turmoil of rival needs, economic upheaval, two world wars, and the use of the Rue de Lille building as a center for the French Baptist Federation led to the dispersal of members to other churches. However, after the Second World War, French Baptists reactivated the Rue de Lille building's role as an office and literature center for French Baptists. In 1956 the nucleus of believers worshiping there were

recognized as a church. Today, if you visit the
building at 48 Rue de Lille, you will still find the
offices of the French Baptist Federation there, and
their bookstore. And you will also note that two
other congregations besides the French also so worship there--one Chinese and the other Romanian.
They are all small congregations. But all have excellent ministries.

Take for example, the Romanian congregation:
its pastor, in addition to serving his people in
Paris, prepares nine broadcasts a week for the
churches in Romania. In visits to Baptist churches
in Romania, he became aware of their need for a new
hymnal. The project took almost ten years to bring
to fruition, since it required the advice and counsel of church leaders and musicians from all parts
of the country. In 1978 there were 17,000 copies
of the hymnal, with music, distributed among the
churches with the accord of the Romanian Baptist
Union.

Hopes for permission to distribute and finance
a second edition of 10,000 copies are presently the
subject of prayer of this pastor. This is the first
printing of a new hymnal for the over 160,000 Baptists in Romania. The edition is small compared to
the need. But God used a pastor of a tiny emigrant
congregation in Paris which had been offered hospi-
tality by a French Baptist church to answer the
prayers of their brethren in Romania.

So the seeds planted by past generations and by
the present are bearing fruit. We can count it a
privilege to share in the vital ministry of the
French Baptists. Perhaps you would like to join
with them in their prayer that they may be able to
establish a witness in every French "Department" by
the end of the century. Although French Baptists
represent only a small minority of the Christians

167

in France, they long to see France once again redis-
cover that faith which redeems life and makes all
men brothers. But this time let it be done in the
spirit of Christ, and not as a means to consolidate
the power of the state.

(BELGIUM)

Belgian Baptists in 1980 counted 510 members in
ten churches. None of these churches are found in
French-speaking areas, but the three strongest congregations are either English- or Polish-language
churches. One small church uses French, but is found
in a German-language area in Belgium. No Baptist
churches are found in Flanders. In 1970 there were
about 300 Belgian Baptists. On the face of it, the
growth between 1970 and 1980 appears like a tremendous percentage gain. In point of fact, most of this
number represents growth among English-language members.

What changes have there been over the past decade? Basically they have been those of consolida-
tion and preparation. The beginning of the decade
marked the transition of the last churches from
rental to ownership of their own buildings. Secondly, for the first time in their history, instead of
appealing for help exclusively from the outside,
Belgian churches established a home mission board
and contribute both funds and time to its work.
They also have begun to contribute to foreign missions and Baptist World Relief. At the present time
they are standardizing their approach to ordination,
recognizing the fact that their pastors must support
themselves by outside activities. And finally, Baptists seem to have become more open in the past decade to other Protestants and to Roman Catholics.
Historically they had often experienced social con-
demnation as a sect by both wings of the Christian

church, and such memories die slowly. But pulpits
are exchanged and united efforts to reach those outside the church take place today.

As you may know, Belgian Baptists came into
being in the last century as a result of contact
with French Baptists. Up until World War I, Baptist
congregations were a part of the French Baptist Federation, and most of their pastors were French. By
the time of World War I, their number was several
times what it is today. That war, however, saw the
churches separated by battle lines, churches and
homes destroyed, and people displaced who never returned. At the close of the war France was devas-
tated, and French Baptists were no longer able to
assist their Belgian brethren as they had in the
past. Belgian congregations, too, had been devas-
tated, but even so they were considerably stronger
than today. They felt that the time had come in
1922 to form the Belgian Baptist Union. In 1939
World War II broke over the countryside, and once
again families and congregations were dispersed both
by the war and the occupation. The churches emerged
from their war experience decimated and fragile.

American Baptists, through their fraternal representatives, provided assistance to both Baptists
and the general population after both wars, and have
tried to undergird Belgian Baptist efforts to re-
establish their ministry and outreach without assuming their responsibility for witness in their country. Although our relationship is, along with the
French, the oldest, our support is channeled through
the Belgian Committee of the European Baptist Federation. Under the chairmanship of the European
General Secretary, representatives from Belgium,
France, The Netherlands, Germany, and the United
States (one each from the Southern and American Baptists) meet annually to select, after due prayer and
consideration, those projects which collectively

meet Belgian priorities and available resources.

What are the problems and what should be done about them? Basically, the churches need to be strengthened and their witness needs to become national.

In terms of strength, the churches are too small and too few to reap the benefit of their labor. The youth raised in their congregations leave home and the area for work, studies, or marriage when they become adults. By and large these young people make excellent contributions to the churches they join in their new communities. But their effectiveness is lost for Baptists. The resident adults who decide to join Baptist churches barely replace the diminishing older generation. As a result, local church growth is very slow. There are two potential responses--one is evangelistic outreach and the other is merger with a larger body of like-minded Christians. Belgian Baptists have only practiced the former. Usually this consists of missions conducted by the local members in their community. More recently they have invited nationals from other countries to share this witness.

In the last few years, groups of French-speaking young people from the U.S., Britain, and Canada (Quebec) have formed teams for united efforts in individual churches. This has always borne fruit and has accelerated growth. However, there are also Free Churches in Belgium whose expression of faith and church structure are very similar to Baptists. They practice believer's baptism; they practice congregational direction of the local church; and they recognize specialized ministries, such as the pastorate and the diaconate. They recognize the Scripture as their final authority in matters of faith and doctrine, and the right of each person to be faithful to his or her own conscience in response to God and his Word. They tend to differ from us in not seeking association in the larger church. These churches are much more numerous than those in the Belgian Baptist Union. Perhaps it may be God's will that these churches collectively pool their efforts to become more effective stewards of the gifts that God has given to each.

In terms of national outreach, the German frontier churches have always expressed an interest in ministry to the German-language area of Belgium. But they believe the initiative and direction must arise within Belgium. So far no German-speaking Belgian has responded to this need. In the Flemish area, however, a number of interesting developments have taken place. Independent Flemish congregations have approached the Belgian Baptist Union, but so far have had reservations about formal association because of the language difference. Secondly, individual Flemish men have responded to God's call and completed or are completing studies for the ministry, and they have asked the Belgian Union if they would be prepared to sponsor them. These seem to indicate that the time has come for Belgian Baptists to expand their ministry into Flanders.

In the recent past, the Roman Catholic faith became so intimately associated with Belgian identity that failure to accept it was seen as a betrayal of cultural identity. Certainly the Latin Church deserves full credit for her faithful witness which introduced and nurtured the growth of the Christian faith down through the ages. And no doubt the vast majority of Belgians will continue to find and to express their faith in God through the ministry of this church.

But today there are Belgians who believe in the real presence of Christ in their lives, in worship, and at his table, but they do not believe in the

171

physical transformation of the elements Jesus held up before his disciples at the Last Supper. There are lay people, priests, and nuns who no longer believe that the church has the right to require celibacy of those who hear God's call. And there are those who believe the Primate of that church deserves both respect and a hearing when he speaks on behalf of his church's faith, but they can only accept his teachings as infallible by violating their own conscience before God and his Word. It is to these to whom we minister, saying there is a place for you in the church of Christ. That is why Baptists are in Belgium and why their ministry, insignificant though their number may be, is vital.

And to all those who have not yet experienced God's real presence, Baptists join with all other Christians in sharing the good news that God personally loves them and has the power to work through them for the good of his creation, regardless of life's circumstances, and that he has demonstrated this to all humanity through Jesus Christ, his Son and our Lord.

(THE NETHERLANDS)

Dutch Baptists pride themselves on their independent origins. They are a contemporary example of a phenomenon that seems to have regularly occurred in church history whenever Christians subject their church practices to the light of the Scriptures.

In the nineteenth century the Seminary at Groningen University became renowned for producing, in the spirit of Erasmus as it likes to say, devout and learned Reformed pastors, who sensitized members of their churches to the implications of their faith for every relationship in life. Dr. Johannes Feisser, one of the graduates, was appointed to a wealthy parish in the Groningen area. He became concerned over two issues--baptized unbelievers taking the Lord's Supper and the miserable plight of the peat-bog workers. His reexamination of the teaching of Scripture led him to refuse baptism for children, and as a result he was dismissed. Dr. Feisser continued, however, his work among the deprived.

Baptists in Germany heard of the ministry of this former Reformed pastor and initiated conversations with him. Two years later, Julius Köbner, a Danish associate of the German evangelist, Johann Oncken, baptized Dr. Feisser and six of his colleagues on Sunday, May 15, 1845, at Stadskanaal, Netherlands. The same day, they constituted a Baptist church, and were received into the Baptist Union of Germany and Denmark. In 1881 the Dutch congregations founded the Baptist Union of Churches in The Netherlands. At the end of the century, there were thirteen Dutch Baptist churches.

In 1980 Dutch Baptists had 11,951 members in their congregations. During the year they received 420 people into 81 member churches upon confession of faith and Christian baptism, and supported eight church-extension projects. In 1970 they had 354 baptisms, 9,611 members, and 70 churches. This indicates a growth of 25 percent in membership over the last ten years. In their general work they support several retirement and psychiatric centers, a national church paper, Christian education material, youth work, and home and foreign missions.

Their seminary, de Vinkenhof, in the suburbs of Utrecht, had 28 students in 1980. The Dean, Dr. J. Reiling, is also professor of New Testament at the State University. And the Associate Dean, Pastor T. Van der Laan, is very active in clinical pastoral training in The Netherlands. De Finkenhof has an impact far beyond its immediate student body who enter the pastoral ministry or serve as chaplains and teachers. (American Baptists can be proud to have made a modest contribution in the past to the seminary library fund.) De Vinkenhof does not limit itself to serving the immediate student body. It also serves as a center for large assemblies in the summer months, and the staff works all year long with local churches and associations as resource persons.

In their overseas work, their major emphasis is upon support of the European Baptist Mission which has work in Africa and South America. But even as they work cooperatively with the European Baptist Mission, they have also contributed personnel and funds to American Baptist work in Zaire.

Dutch Baptists share many problems which are common to all the churches in The Netherlands.

There is a rising spirit which has called into question all the traditional social norms. Divorce and separation, currently affecting about one out of every four families, is a relatively new phenomenon which has spawned a host of problems.

Economic recession has left large numbers of unemployed, and it has raised questions for young and old alike over what their role and place can be in today's society. For example, there is currently a surplus of physicians in The Netherlands. So both those with newly acquired skills and those with no skills have found it increasingly difficult to make a meaningful contribution.

The integration of a large immigrant non-European population is a new question for the nation, and there is now an emerging second generation who have only known The Netherlands as home. They will probably have to give up the illusion their parents had about an eventual place for them in their ancestral lands.

With the densest population in Europe, space for their population's family, work, and leisure needs has been a perennial problem, which only exacerbates other social issues.

The churches believe that the allocation of limited resources in terms of priorities which will favor their society's capacity to meet the needs of the nation in a world community is too important a question to abandon to the secularists, but they have not yet found a satisfactory solution.

And finally, the churches face the question of their own relationships in the face of different traditions. Christians are finding that they appear to have more in common with like-minded believers than they may have with other members in their own church. Charismatics feel more comfortable with other charismatics; social activists want to pool their efforts; evangelicals want to reach their neighbor for Christ; and conservatives tend to look for ways to redefine the boundaries of the faith today. Clergy are discovering that their congregations no longer take shelter behind their confessional differences, and the clergy themselves often taking positions which are more appreciated by other Christians than those within their own church body. The divisions within the Roman Catholic Church in The Netherlands appear almost as great as those that separate various Reformed churches. And yet there is as much a desire to maintain unity within one's communion as there is to reach out to formerly estranged Christians. We do not know at this time how these tensions will evolve, but they are there.

Dutch Baptists also face problems arising from their own situation. Their churches have been

strongest in the rural areas, and the transition to
the urban area has been only partially successful.
Urbanization and increased social mobility have
weakened many congregations making it exceedingly
difficult for them to support a full-time ministry.
This generation has seen a sharp upsurge in the num-
of young people entering the professions and manage-
ment, creating a social as well as a generational
gap in local congregations. And the anonymity of
urban life has accentuated isolation and pain in congregations which once knew each other intimately.
Income seems to have reached a relative plateau as
recession and inflation make planning increasingly
difficult.

Dutch Baptists will continue their emphasis on
a personal commitment for Jesus Christ. They are
introducing in 1981 their first study materials de-
signed to bring people together around issues of
faith and life that are common to their age group.
And there is a tendency to turn away from identify-
ing problems as abstract theological or social issues
and address them in terms of how Christians are experiencing these issues in their personal lives.
Evangelism has tended to be approached in the past
rather simplistically, addressing the despair and
inertia of individuals with the promise of salvation
in Christ. Pastors are now beginning to address
"the dark side of life" which does not appear to be
subject to change but for which there is also salvation in Christ. And finally they are moving away
from an emphasis on sharing information about the
Christian life to an emphasis on "formation/teaching,"
or growth through "meeting" one another honestly at
this point in time on their Christian pilgrimage.

Perhaps the best way to summarize the spirit
Dutch pastors are bringing to the next decade is to
quote one of them:

I think when things have gone wrong in
an individual's family, marriage or personal life, I must not try to meet it as
a principle but as a person in pain. I
do not accept abortion or believe in divorce, but I must accept the pain of my
neighbor and meet him there.

Some years ago, social and political engagement appeared to make the Church
more credible, but practically speaking
those churches which emphasize political
involvement are losing their members.
I think "engagement" is only a projection
for sophisticated debate. The real problems are the personal problems of people
in a changing society. People talk about
society, but their problems are personal.

Dutch Baptists are the only mainline denomination in The Netherlands which hasn't suffered a membership loss sometime during the last ten years.
They are the only Baptist body in Western Europe to
have grown during every year this century. With the
tremendous problems facing the churches and their
country, they are not sure they will continue to
receive the same hearing and response from their
compatriots in the coming years. But they want to
be faithful stewards of their share in the proclama-
tion of the gospel and invite you to pray for them
and their people.

(WEST GERMANY)

The "Bundesrepublik Deutschland" (Federal Republic of Germany) is centered directly between
Eastern and Western Europe. Therefore its contribution to detente--along with its sister German State,
the German Democratic Republic (East Germany)--is

significant for the future of peaceful European relations.

The German Baptists are a group of 63,000 out of a population of 61 million. They are officially called Evangelische Frekirchliche Gemeinden (Evangelical Free Churches), because during World War II the German Baptists united with the Pentecostalists and Plymouth Brethren to form the above named union. After the war the Pentecostalists in West Germany left the union, but the Brethren remained.

The German Baptists have assumed leadership positions in the European Baptist Federation and the Baptist World Alliance. Dr. Rudolf Thaut, for many years General Secretary and Seminary Director, was a President of the European Baptist Federation and Vice-President of the Baptist World Alliance. Now Dr. Gerhard Claas, former General Secretary of the German Baptists and of the European Baptist Federation, is the new General Secretary of the Baptist World Alliance in Washington, D.C.

In the 1960s there was a lack of growth among German Baptists, but in the past few years an increased emphasis upon evangelism has resulted in an increase in baptisms and church growth. Tent evangelism is used extensively in the summers. Many large city churches have experimented successfully in new forms of witness, including coffee houses, youth centers, and student houses.

West German Baptists are very social-minded with numerous hospitals and old people's homes, as well as kindergartens. There are several German Baptist deaconess orders, where women commit themselves to a life of service for the churches. They are very helpful not only in hospitals but also in local congregations.

Because of the "Wirtschaftswunder" and economic power of Germany, the German churches are able to be of tremendous assistance financially to the European Baptist Federation. They are particularly helpful in maintaining ties with Eastern Europe.

In 1984 the European Baptist Federation Congress will be held in Hamburg, Germany, and will also celebrate the 150th anniversary of the baptism of Johann Gerhard Oncken, the founder of the German Baptists and missionary to much of Europe. He was baptized by an American Baptist professor from Newton--Professor Barnas Sears. Thus there is a historical relationship between our two conventions.

(AUSTRIA)

Austria is almost 90 percent Catholic, and it has a population of seven and a half million. What can 700 Baptists do as much a minority movement? Actually, it is surprising to see the vitality of the Austrian Baptists. There are basically two large concentrations of Baptists--Salzburg and Vienna. Much of the work among students and young people is centered in these two cities which then influence missions in other parts of the country. Other cities also have strong Baptists congregations, Graz and Linz. New mission work is being attempted in Innsbruck and Bad Ischl.

The history of Austrian Protestantism is very interesting for us, since during the Reformation Austria became almost totally Anabaptist and was influenced by the great Anabaptist leader, Balthasar Humbaier, whose famous lecture ended, "The Truth is immortal." Austrian Baptists look to these roots for inspiration and are increasingly gaining confidence to witness among the many alienated young people in their midst. Austria is a prosperous society; and, although nominally religious, there is a great longing among young people for meaning in life. Ski retreats and summer programs are attractive means of trying to reach the young.

The European Baptist Federation tries to help the small Baptist union by sponsoring an Austrian Mission Committee which overlooks financial matters and attempts to give direction to mission programs.

(SWITZERLAND)

Neutral Switzerland might seem to be neutral also about religion, since half of its population is Catholic and the other half Protestant. Switzerland was the center of two outstanding reformations—the French-speaking Reformation of John Calvin in Geneva and the German-speaking Reformation of Ulrich Zwingli. Beautiful Alps and mountain scenery give the tourist a feeling of well-being and that all is peaceful. Actually, recent demonstrations by the young people show that a remarkable number of the students are alienated from their rich and materially well-off country. There is little unemployment, no poverty, good education, almost idyllic settings for recreation and fun. Yet, something is missing. Less than 6 percent attend church, and yet the majority are members of the state churches—either Catholic or Reformed.

The Baptists of Switzerland number only 1,500 (German-speaking) and thus are quite a minority, particularly in a country so influenced by the Reformation. (There is a group of French-speaking Baptists numbering about 1,000; but they do not belong to the Baptist World Alliance, and we have little contact with them.) The Swiss Baptists, in spite of their small number, are well recognized. They are members of the Swiss National Council of Churches and have good contacts with other churches, usually participating with all groups in a week of prayer.

The largest church among the Baptists is Salemskappelle in Zurich with a membership of 700—almost half of the Baptists of German-speaking Switzerland! The church in Zurich has an amazing witness and outreach. It has forty house groups which form the main mission arm of the church. They are open to new ideas and very supportive of other Baptist groups. On one Sunday they collected $15,000 for victims of the earthquake in Romania.

The influence of Swiss Baptists is increased by the presence of the Baptist Theological Seminary in Rüschlikon. This seminary has students from 20 countries in Europe and overseas. It has a well-rounded European and American faculty. It is really the graduate seminary for Baptists in Europe, having about 60 students.

Dr. James L. Sprigg
BIM Fraternal Representative
Central and Eastern Europe
Rüschlikon, Switzerland

181

EASTERN EUROPE

Background of Eastern European Baptists Today
Denton Lotz

The Baptist witness in Eastern Europe is strong. Two-thirds of the Baptists in Europe live in this geographical area. There are many terms used in the West to describe Eastern Europe. Some people speak of "behind the iron curtain," others speak of the "communist countries," and still others more moderately speak of the "socialist countries." The use of the geographical term "Eastern Europe" is perhaps least emotional and best suited for Baptist purposes.

When we speak of Eastern Europe, we are referring to the following countries: German Democratic Republic, Czechoslovakia, Bulgaria, Hungary, Poland, Romania, U.S.S.R., and Yugoslavia. The peoples in these countries are made up of myriad cultures, languages, and customs. They are not a monolithic group. The languages include Germanic, Slavic, Romance, and more. Their religious affiliations traditionally include Catholic, Orthodox, Lutheran, Reformed, and a small group of Free Churches--the majority are called Baptists.

What we want to mention briefly here is that which makes Eastern Europe a special entity today. What is it that unites Eastern Europe as a geographical designation and goes beyond this? The answer should be obvious! I am referring to the form of government, the ideology that is common all the above-mentioned countries. Marxist-Leninism is the ideology which unites the various governments. This ideology is maintained in its various expressions by the Communist Party which basically controls the major decisions and philosophy of government. It is not the intent of this article to analyze this system of government but to affirm that the Christian church, and more specifically the Baptists, lives and witnesses under this ideology and this form of government. We shall do this by answering briefly some questions often asked about Eastern Europe.

Eye-Witness Answers for Some Misperceptions

"Do they have freedom?" The Germans have a word, "jaein," which is a combination of yes (ja) and no (nein), thus "jaein" (yes/no). The answer to the question of freedom is no easy "yes" or "no," because the question is more complicated than we at first might assume! What do we mean by freedom? Do we mean our Western concept of freedom? Our American concept? If we do, then we will have difficulties understanding the "freedom" of an Eastern European. In fact we would be inclined to say: "They have no freedom!" But, if we ask the question from the point of view of an unemployed person in South America who sees freedom in the light of employment, then the Eastern European has a lot of freedom--maybe too much! If, in Somalia, we ask the question in the light of a starving mother who has no food and views the question in the light of freedom to eat, then the Eastern European has much freedom in comparison to her lot. Similarly one could ask the question from a point of view of medical services, education, social security, etc. You see, when we discuss the political question of freedom it becomes complicated because of one's own personal experience.

The question with which Christians are most concerned is that of religious freedom. Here I think we need to make the distinction between freedom of religion and freedom of worship. In the Western view religious freedom means the institutional expression of one's faith beyond the four

183

walls of the church. This includes the freedom to have publishing houses, printing presses, orphanages, nursery schools, colleges, universities, hospitals, and access to radio and television. This is the large view of religious freedom. The Baptists in Eastern Europe have some of these freedoms in some instances, but they do not always have all of these freedoms.

What Baptists and other Christians in Eastern Europe have is what I would call the more limited concept of "freedom of worship." This includes the freedom of Christians to assemble for prayer, singing, and preaching--in most cases three times on Sunday and once during the week. The situation varies from country to country. Thus, it's difficult to generalize and to say that all of Eastern Europe is like this or that.

The Polish Baptists publish five books a year in the Polish language, and they have access to the Bible Society which has a store in downtown Warsaw. The Baptists in the German Democratic Republic (GDR) run a hospital for retarded children. The Hungarian Baptists have a youth camp on a beautiful lake for summer retreats, etc. Most of the Baptists have seminaries (except the U.S.S.R. which has a correspondence course, but they are praying for permission to open a seminary in Moscow soon). Some pastors, e.g., in Czechoslovakia, have their salaries paid by the state. As one can see, the situation differs from country to country.

Basically, Baptists are free to preach and free to worship in their buildings. Opportunities are limited beyond that, although there are exceptions-- the Polish Baptists make their own broadcasts sent out over Trans World Radio (TWR), and Baptists in the German Democratic Republic occasionally are permitted to broadcast worship services over the state radio.

It should be clear that Baptists in Eastern
Europe do not have the freedoms that we have in the
U.S.A. This is obvious. Yet, the church continues
to grow and witness—more than in the West! Beyond
the political question of freedom, the Christian
really is concerned about a much greater question
of freedom--spiritual freedom, freedom in Christ!
Paul said in 2 Corinthians 3:17, "Where the Spirit
of the Lord is, there is freedom."

One man I met in Romania was the most vile and
evil man in town. He had killed another man. He
beat up his wife who had to be hospitalized. After
being let out of prison he married another woman and
beat her up. She went to a little Baptist chapel
and found Christ as Savior. She told the members
about her husband. They prayed for him. One night
he had been drinking and fell down in the snow. A
policeman found him in his drunken state and asked
him where he lived, since he would die if he were
out in the snow all night. He was in front of his
own home! When he went inside he saw his wife on
her knees praying for him. He became so angry that
he grabbed a knife and moved to kill her, but he
tripped over her feet and ended on the floor crying
like a baby. That next Sunday he went to the chapel
and gave his heart to Christ. He became a free person! Now I wish you could see him, traveling all
over town on his little moped telling of his new
life to all his old drinking buddies. If you asked
him, "Do you have freedom?" he would say, "Yes, I
have freedom because I've met Christ, the Liberator."
This is the biblical question of freedom. It is a
freedom against which no one can build walls or make
laws or restrict: "Where the Spirit of the Lord is,
there is freedom."

"Do they have Bibles?" The availability of
Bibles varies from country to country. The two
places where Bibles are most needed in Eastern Europe

are in the U.S.S.R. and Romania. Why? Because that is where the church is growing the most. There is really a revival going on in many places within these two countries. Therefore, new believers need Bibles. Otherwise, one could use one's grandfather's Bible. In most other countries of Eastern Europe it is relatively easy to purchase a Bible. German Bibles are readily available in East Berlin--sold openly in the Baptist bookstore. In Czechoslovakia a new edition of the Bible has just been printed, more than 140,000. The 4,200 Baptists received more than 5,000 Bibles--more than enough for all their members, and some to use in evangelism. Also, in Hungary and Yugoslavia there is no problem in getting a Bible. In Poland the British and Foreign Bible Society has a store and stockroom in downtown Warsaw. After Billy Graham's meetings in Poland the store has been flooded with requests for Bibles. The situation is difficult in Bulgaria for the 600 Baptists. Opportunities are severely limited. In the U.S.S.R. and Romania the United Bible Societies has used diplomatic efforts, along with the Baptist World Alliance, to get permission to either import or print Bibles there.

In December, 1979, I had the privilege of seeing many of the 20,000 new Bibles printed in Leningrad distributed at the council meeting of the All Union Council of Evangelical Christians-Baptists (AUCECB). This is not enough. In fact, Brother Bichkov, General Secretary of the Russian Baptists, dreams of one day getting one million Bibles into the U.S.S.R. In Romania we have often had opportunity to speak with government officials, and over the past few years 10,000 Bibles have been imported. This is not enough, but it is a beginning. It is a policy of the American Bible Society not to smuggle, but to work through diplomatic channels. As American Baptist representative to Eastern Europe, this was also the policy we adopted, and we found it to be more honest and more helpful for other aspects of the church's mission in the long view of history.

One more thing remains to be said about the Bible in Eastern Europe. Biblical faith has been preserved to a remarkable degree precisely because of various limitations. The Holy Spirit has worked through biblical preaching to preserve and to enlarge a believing church faithful to the gospel!

"What about theological education?" Baptists today believe that an educated ministry is desirable for the nurture of the church. Yet, miraculously at times, the Baptist witness has often grown without educated pastors. It was the laity in Europe, East and West, that first carried the Baptist call for biblical conversion. Colporteurs handed out Bibles. Merchants on trips around Europe started prayer cells. Believers met in homes and sometimes secretly in the forest during the nineteenth century, lest the state churches persecute them--be the state church Catholic, Orthodox, Lutheran, or Reformed! The great "apostle to the peasants" among Baptists in Hungary was Kornya, a man who had only a second grade education, and yet he baptized more than 10,000 persons.

However, as the Baptist witness grew, the believers realized that they needed also to grow in the faith, and they needed teachers and educated pastors. Thus, Baptist seminaries sprang up all over Europe. Even today these seminaries continue to function in most countries. Some of them operate on a more modest scale than before World War II. For example, in Romania before the war there were 120 students. Now, there are thirty students in Bucharest's seminary. Nevertheless, the leaders rejoice that they at least have a seminary. The Germans used to send all their students to Hamburg, but with the division of the country those living in the

German Democratic Republic (East Germany) were allowed to start a new seminary in Buckow. This seminary is flourishing, with exchange students even from Estonia in the U.S.S.R.! It is rewarding to see the number of young Polish Baptists who study at the Evangelical Academy in Warsaw and then take Baptist courses at their own seminary. The Hungarian Baptist Seminary in Budapest has always had a standard of excellence. Today its professors are capable and have graduate degrees. The Baptists in Czechoslovakia do not have a seminary but send their students to the Comenius Faculty of the Reformed Church in Prague. Because not always enough students are able to attend, correspondence courses are offered. The U.S.S.R. does not have a seminary. However, Russian Baptists are allowed to have a pastor-training correspondence course with more than 100 pastors enrolled. The Russian believers are praying that their application to open a seminary will be approved, since they are the only Baptists in Eastern Europe without a seminary, except for the small group of believers in Bulgaria!

The European Baptist Federation sponsors a Summer Institute of Theological Education (SITE) held each summer on the campus of the Baptist Theological Seminary in Rüschlikon. It was a particular joy for me to found and direct the SITE program for two years. Pastors from all over Eastern Europe came for four weeks of study and fellowship. A mini-library of good-quality theological books is given to each student. I wish you could see the joy and tears of the students when they receive these outstanding books. They are able to take these back home without any problems! International Ministries shares in supporting this project.

"Are there any young people in the churches?" In Eastern Europe the churches are crowded with young people. This is true whether in Poland or

Romania or the Soviet Union. Christ speaks to the needs of young people, and the philosophy of dialectical materialism is not meeting the deepest longing of the human heart. Youth choirs are particularly inspiring in the Soviet Union. Whether in the Ukraine, Moscow, or the Baltic states, beautiful singing from many young people is refreshing to hear. In Poland there are teams of guitar-playing young people who visit the churches and help in evangelization. There are various youth programs. For example, in Yugoslavia there is a camp off the coast of Zadar where all the summer teams of young people come, set up their tents, and have Bible.studies and fun. BIM was instrumental in providing funds for the purchase of the property.

Sunday school varies from country to country. The Russians, for example, never had the tradition of Sunday school, since under the Czars the Baptists were restricted much more than today. Thus in the U.S.S.R. religious education is almost completely carried on in the family. On the other hand, in Poland one can see Sunday school classes meeting on Sunday morning during worship.

"Can they evangelize?" Johann Gerhard Oncken, the great leader of the German Baptists who organized much of Baptist work in Eastern Europe in the nineteenth century, once said, "Jeder Baptist ein Missionar"--"every Baptist a missionary." It is this spirit that continues today. Evangelism is not something left up to the pastor. Everyone is involved in sharing one's faith. A government official asked a Baptist pastor in Romania how the Baptists were able to get so many out to their meetings. He replied, "We tell a blind, deaf, old lady that tomorrow an evangelist is coming, and the church is full!" This illustrates the point that no matter what the age, the Christian faith must be shared with others.

One could give countless illustrations of men
and women who in their daily life have been effective witnesses to new life in Christ. One man
worked in a bus factory and was going home after his
shift. He saw that another worker was having trou-
ble and stopped to help him. The worker was surprised at his help and said, "Why do you help me?"
The Baptist replied, "Because I'm a believer." The
worker asked to go to church with the believer.
Through this means of witness, the Baptist was able
to lead eight other men to Christ. All aspects of
the worship service encourage the sharing of one's
faith. The beautiful singing and choirs are incredible all over Eastern Europe. A communist professor
told me that she very often stood outside the Baptist church just to hear the beautiful singing!

Many churches have special services for evangelism in the springtime, like some churches in the
U.S.A. Friends are invited, tracts handed out, and
prayer meetings held in homes preparing for these
meetings. The visit of foreigners from abroad is
always an opportunity for evangelism. That is why
many believers in Eastern Europe are discouraged
when pastors from the West bring only short devotional messages and not evangelistic sermons calling
for commitment to Christ. Every occasion, whether
a wedding or a funeral, is used to announce the joyous news of God's love in Christ.

"What type of contact do you have with the
government?" This question has often been directed
to me. As official representative of the American
Baptist International Ministries, it soon developed
that one of my tasks was to visit various government
officials. This was a very interesting aspect of my
work. There are those who think that we should have
no contact with the communists. This is very unrealistic, and in fact not a Christian attitude, I
feel. As American Baptists we have nothing to hide

in establishing contact with our Baptist friends in
Eastern Europe.

The advantages of diplomatic contacts with the
government are numerous. First of all it establishes
credibility with the government and our brethren in
these countries. Those who smuggle and think that
going "underground" is the best way to help our
brethren miss a very important opportunity to witness. By establishing good contacts with the government, we are able to discuss issues very important
to the local Baptist groups. We can help to encourage government permission to build new churches, to
get scholarships for students, to secure visas for
pastors to study in the West, and to seek permission
to print books or import Bibles. The Christian
church has lived under various forms of government
these past 2,000 years. None of these forms of government should be equated with divine rule! All of
them have the seeds of sin in them because they are
dominated by sinful men and women. Yet all have
the potential to do good because God works through
and in spite of man's stubborness.

On many occasions when talking with government
officials I have had the opportunity to witness to
faith in Christ. One official asked, "Why are you
a Christian?" This was a wonderful opportunity to
explain the gospel and to tell him, "I love Christ,
and I love you and pray for you." The translator
did not believe I would want to say that, but I did.
Since then I have prayed for this man. Does not
the Bible remind us to pray for those in authority?
Are we not encouraged to witness wherever we are?
A pastor in the German Democratic Republic once
preached a sermon in which he said that the conversion of the Apostle Paul almost failed because of
the Christians. The early Christians could not believe that a persecutor of the church could have
found faith! The pastor went on to say, "How do we

know that God is not raising up another apostle among communist leaders? Would we in the church be prepared to receive him?"

Scandals and evil in government are not limited to only one system of government--recent history has proven that! All Christians are called upon to witness to Christ within the various structures in which we live. I remember a student once asking a Russian Baptist leader, "What will happen after Breznhev?" The leader replied, "We did not ask what would happen after Khruschev. We know that the future belongs to Jesus Christ, and that is enough to give us hope to live now and to witness now." It is this faith in the future with Christ that should guide all of us in our various contacts with governments around the world.

"What have we done?" In visiting various American churches it always surprises me to see how little many people know about what International Ministries has done in Eastern Europe. I would venture to say that American Baptists, along with the Baptist World Alliance and Southern Baptists, have done more for our Baptists in Eastern Europe than all the various publicized "underground-church" groups put together!

BUILDINGS: In America when we build, we usually hire a contractor and pay for construction. Then we have a beautiful building. In Eastern Europe, it is not that way. In fact, the church members themselves sacrifice many hours after their normal work to build their own churches. This is true whether in Czechoslovakia, Poland, or the U.S.S.R., and other countries. But building supplies are often needed and funds are not always available for this. Thus, International Ministries has helped with funds for many buildings in most countries of Eastern Europe. I wish you could be at a dedication ceremony of some of these buildings. In Arad, Romania, more than 5,000 persons were present, and what a joyous occasion it was! The service began at 8 o'clock in the morning with an orchestra and a choir singing the "Hallelujah Chorus." The preaching, singing, poetry, and orchestral celebration lasted until 10 o'clock in the evening, with breaks for lunch and supper. More than 2,000 persons were fed in the basement of the huge new church building. There are now more permits for building new churches in Eastern Europe than we in International Ministries and the Baptist World Alliance can support. Therefore, contributions for this are always received with gratefulness by our believing friends in Eastern Europe.

SCHOLARSHIPS FOR TRAVEL: Many times when you meet a believer from Eastern Europe at a Baptist World Alliance meeting or an American Baptist Churches biennial convention you might not realize that his travel was made possible by International Ministries. This is one important way that we are able to help. Many of the Eastern European brothers and sisters long for the opportunity to visit their believing friends in the West. Visas are available but funds are not. For this reason the Baptist World Alliance has just established a scholarship fund for traveling.

RADIO BROADCASTING: Every day International Ministries helps support a radio evangelist broadcasting into Romania. Jeremie Hodoroaba lives in Paris and broadcasts over Trans World Radio. These broadcasts cost a lot of money. International Ministries helps make this possible by working through a committee of the Romanian Church in Paris.

MEDICAL AID: Very often there are medicines in the West which are urgently needed for emergency treatment. Or, it might be that a cripple from a certain country can best be operated on in West Germany. All of this costs money and again International Ministries is there to help.

STUDY GRANTS: SITE, the Summer Institute of Theological Education, in Rüschlikon, is a project of the European Baptist Federation. The mini-library, travel, cost of four weeks' lodging and food are expensive. Our study grants help make it possible for many pastors to attend. In addition to this International Ministries helps the various seminaries in their own countries.

BIBLES AND BOOKS: The recent printing of 20,000 Bibles in Leningrad was partially supported by International Ministries funds granted to the European Baptist Federation. Also, when Bibles were sent by the United Bible Society to Romania, we helped out. In addition to this, many books are sent to seminaries and pastors from our offices in Switzerland. Also, many pastors who have traveled to the West are able to bring books back with them.

AUTOMOBILES FOR PASTORS: Sometimes a pastor serves ten little congregations. To take a bus would require many hours and waste time. Through International Ministries aid we have been able to help pastors purchase automobiles, aiding them in their ministries.

The list could go on, but this should be enough to convince you that much has already been done and that more can be done. The offerings and sacrifices of American congregations are greatly appreciated by the churches in Eastern Europe.

Baptist Church Life in Marxist-Leninist
Eastern Europe

It is impossible in so short a space to give an

Romanian Baptists are noted for their music—vocal and instrumental—and their bands play both gospel melodies and Bach.

The Baptist Book Store in East Berlin indicates the availability of Christian literature in one communist country.

in-depth report on the life of each Baptist Union in Eastern Europe. I will try to highlight aspects of the Baptist witness in the various countries, and in this way give a feeling for the everyday witness of the churches.

(BULGARIA)

The Baptists in Bulgaria comprise the smallest of the Baptist conventions (or unions) in Eastern Europe. There are only 600 Baptists in Bulgaria, yet their churches are vital and a good number of young people attend. At the Baptist church in Sophia, I was pleased to see a good group of young people with courage and an unbelievable faith in a difficult situation.

Bulgaria for many centuries was dominated by the Muslim invaders from Turkey. The Orthodox Church was the one uniting factor during this period of occupation. Thus, the Orthodox Church is greatly respected among the populace as the preserver and bearer of Bulgarian tradition. This has positive and negative aspects. It gives a certain loyalty to the church. On the other hand, when the church becomes too strongly a cultural bearer, it loses its evangelistic zeal. The small group of Baptists from Sophia to Varna on the Black Sea, and Plovdiv in the central region, are a reminder that evangelism is at the heart of the Christian faith.

Plovdiv is a beautiful city that goes back to the time of Philip of Macedonia. He had wanted to make this his capital! When Paul heard the cry "Come over into Macedonia and help us," little did he realize that centuries later, north of Macedonia, there would be a little Baptist church on May 1st Street. It was moving to speak in a packed little upper room to 125 people. The electricity went out while I was preaching in German, and I spoke in the dark for a while until a candle was brought. It was symbolic to me of how the church witnesses in a dark world. Often we see more darkness than light, but then a candle is lit and darkness disappears and new hope appears. It was moving to listen to the testimony of a young student who left family and security to follow Christ. What a beautiful witness she was to the courage that Christ can give.

Bulgarian Baptists have not participated in the European Baptist Federation and Baptist World Alliance as much as many of us had hoped. Recent invitations and discussions with the government have expressed the interest of Baptists around the world for a more visible representation of Bulgarian Baptists at our international meetings.

(CZECHOSLOVAKIA)

The symbol of the Baptists of Czechoslovakia is that of a communion cup over an open Bible. This identifies Baptists with the long tradition of Reformed faith in that country, going back to Huss. It is a wonderful tradition, including the faith of those who lived in Moravia and Bohemia.

Today Baptists number 3,917. It has not been easy for them to evangelize in a country which has a strong Reformed tradition. There are large Baptist churches in Prague, Bratislava, and Brno. Through invitation to Bible study and worship services, the Baptists endeavor to reach a very secular society. A number of the pastors are well educated, having studied at the theological faculty of the university--the Comenius Faculty.

The recent publication of a new translation of the Bible has given new impetus to Bible study.

This new translation was done in the country and printed there with ample numbers for every Baptist.

The church in Bratislava has been able to purchase an old Lutheran church in town and has beautifully restored it. Statistics are always very deceptive. For example, in one town in Czechoslovakia there are 20,000 Lutherans, and 2,000 may be in church on Sunday. Of the 2,000 Reformed, there may be 20 in the services. The 300 Baptists of Bratislava, when they meet on Sunday, usually have 500. Thus the spiritual dynamic of the Baptist work is greater than their numbers would indicate.

Rev. Stanislav Svec is General Secretary of the Baptist Union of Czechoslovakia and is serving now as Vice-President of the European Baptist Federation. Next year his leadership as President of the European Baptist Federation will be a good indication to Christians around the world of how the barrier between East and West has been broken in Baptist life! All Baptists in Europe try to work together in whatever way possible.

A strong youth work involving study groups and choirs adds to the fellowship that the youth enjoy among Baptists in Czechoslovakia.

(GERMAN DEMOCRATIC REPUBLIC)

The 23,000 Baptists of the Deutsche Demokratische Republik (more commonly known as East Germany) are a distinct and separate Baptist Union from their brethren in the West. They have their own leadership, seminary, publishing house, social work, etc.

One particularly interesting part of the work of Baptists in the German Democratic Republic is their retreat center in Schmiedeberg. It is called

Martin Luther King Haus, named that with the permission of Mrs. Coretta King. It is a sign to all that Baptists have a social concern in their Christian faith. The building is a beautiful retreat center with 160 beds and is used for men's retreats, as well as women's meeting, youth retreats, or ecumenical seminars. It was built entirely by the Baptists in the area and serves a real need for Christians in the whole of the country.

I was at a retreat there which included laity and pastors from Scandinavia and most countries of Eastern Europe. The fellowship and study together were highlights of spiritual growth for many of those who attended. Baptist witness in the German Democratic Republic extends from the Baltic to the South where it borders on Czechoslovakia. Thus, Baptists in this part of Germany are really a link between Baptists in East and West. Their theological education is in the good German tradition of historical theology, biblical studies, and practical theology. They read the same literature as their counterparts in the West, yet they live in a socialist environment. I feel that the Baptists in the German Democratic Republic are making a significant contribution as a bridge.

One of the joys recently was to visit the new building in progress in East Berlin. The Bethel Baptist Church was bombed out during World War II, and the members were never able to rebuilt. Now they are building a huge structure which will be a tremendous benefit to all of the Baptists in that country. Hundreds of Baptists have worked on this. The young and old had to dig a ditch for 300 yards on a busy street to lay an electrical cable. By their work all of the neighborhood soon learned who they were and what kind of building was going up. Through the Baptist World Alliance, American Baptists have made a significant contribution to this building.

(HUNGARY)

When the Baptist World Alliance met in Stockholm, Sweden, in 1975, Baptists from around the world marveled at the beautiful singing of the Baptist choir from Budapest, Hungary. Anyone who has visited Hungary would not have been surprised. The Hungarian Baptists have beautiful choirs in all of their churches. Many who sing in them are professional singers and musicians. The Christian faith is communicated not only through preaching but also through the sung word. This is certainly true in Hungary.

The Hungarian Baptists began through the witness of a merchant from Hamburg named Rottmayer who visited Budapest in 1847. The small Baptists community endured much hardship, their churches were burned, their pastors imprisoned, and the believers persecuted. Nevertheless, as reported earlier, the churches grew, and more than 10,000 were baptized by the "Apostle to the Peasants," Kornya. Today the community of 12,350 Baptists in Hungary are leaders in the Free Church Council. They have an excellent seminary, a retreat center on beautiful Lake Balaton, and churches throughout the country.

Recently permission has been granted for the reconstruction or building of twenty churches. The congregations are eagerly sacrificing their time and energy to complete this project with the help of the Baptist World Alliance. In 1978 Billy Graham spoke in many cities in Hungary--for the first time in a socialist country of Eastern Europe. 20,000 came to the youth camp at Tahi. It was a great ecumenical experience. Today the aftereffects are still being felt in many churches. The young people have a zeal to witness and pastors are searching for new ways to evangelize.

(POLAND)

For many years the American Baptists have been related to the Baptists in Poland. At the beginning of the century we were involved in their seminary in the northern part of the country.

Today there are 2,539 Baptists in Poland. This might not seem like many in a country of 35 million which is very strongly Catholic. Yet anyone who has visited Poland and worshiped with the Baptists comes away with the feeling of having visited a dynamic and young church. There are new Baptist church buildings all over Poland from the mountains in Krynica to the Baltic Sea town of Gdansk. It is an amazing story of faith, for Baptists have really covered the country with small mission stations and churches.

One might ask what the Baptist witness would be in such a strong Roman Catholic country? Actually, it is a witness to the New Testament concept of a believer's church. The Baptists are a reminder to their Catholic neighbors that being a Christian is more than merely having your name on a church roll. It means a living experience of Christ.

When Billy Graham visited Poland in 1979 no one knew what to expect. The Catholic churches were opened to him. In Katowice where the largest cathedral in Poland is to be found, Billy Graham preached to more than 12,000. It was packed with many priests and nuns also attending. The bishop introduced Graham and said, "We want to hear him because he preaches Christ, and we need to hear more about him." Still today people are requesting Bibles all over Poland as a result of this evangelization. It was a great day for Protestants in Poland. It encouraged them and gave them a sense of unity and new purpose.

A beautiful, new old-people's home has just been opened next to the new church building in Bialystok. This is in itself an outstanding witness of God's grace. In 1945 there were only 30 Baptists in this town. Today the congregation of 300 is a combination of many wonderful people--ranging from laborers to artisans, and engineers to 15 medical doctors. International Ministries has been involved in these buildings from their inception.

In 1980 the SITE program in Rüschlikon, Switzerland, had nine students from Poland, including one professor who taught New Testament. The young pastors of Poland are an encouragement to all of us. Many have secular jobs during the week, and they carry on a full-time pastoral responsibility.

(ROMANIA)

At the turn of the century there were not very many Romanian Baptists--perhaps fewer than a thousand. Today there are more than 160,000. It is an experience just to visit one of their churches. The packed churches and the people's emotion in singing and praying cannot be forgotten. Whether in Bucharest, the capital, or in Constanza on the Black Sea, or in Sibiu in the mountains, the churches are so filled that one can only find standing room!

What are the reasons for this tremendous growth in Romania as compared to, say, Poland? Are they more spiritual, or more dynamic? The answer is defino. I met an African Christian and we were discussing this question of church growth. He said, "The Spirit blows where he wants to." Herein ultimately the answer lies. It is a mystery why one people or culture experiences revival at one time and why another people does at another time.

Wherever one goes to Baptist churches in Romania one finds dynamic groups of young people. And they are very educated, many of them studying at the university, in either medicine, engineering, or music, etc. This presents a problem. In the 1,100 Baptist churches there are only 160 pastors, many of whom are not on the same educational level. When a church grows in revival as quickly as in Romania, there are periods of adjustment for new members and old leaders. Romania is now in this situation. The European Baptist Federation tries to help in various ways. One wonderful experience was the meeting of the European Baptist Federation Executive Committee in Bucharest--the first ever in Romania! Thousands came for an opening service where there were more than twenty greetings, many of them sermons from the foreign visitors. Needless to say, the service lasted hours, but with movement and much joy. The brass bands, choirs, and fervent preaching keep one awake!

Many times I have told the story of the Romanian gypsy lady who went into a Baptist church and was so overjoyed at the good news of Christ that she went into the streets and restaurants and everywhere telling people, "God loves you," "Jesus loves you." One man slapped her on the face. The old gypsy lady replied, "In the name of Jesus I forgive you." Again she was slapped, and again she forgave him. She was beat up until she was found on the floor of the railroad station almost dead. Some believers found her and brought her back to her apartment. After three months she got better, and everyone forgot about it. The next year a man came by her apartment and wanted to speak with her. When he came in, he asked, "Don't you know me?" She replied that she did not. Then he said, "I'm the man that beat you up, and every time I hit you, you said 'In the name of Jesus, I forgive you.' I couldn't sleep for three months day or night until I went to a chapel and gave my heart to Christ." Such is the witness of a simple person who can be used mightily of God.

The Romanian Baptists continue to grow and each year baptize almost 10,000 new members.

(U.S.S.R.)

The 545,000 Baptists of the Soviet Union are the largest Baptist group in Europe. Next to the U.S.A. and India, they represent the largest group of Baptists in the world. It is a dynamic movement that covers all of the Soviet Union's fifteen republics from Tallin, Estonia, and Riga, Latvia, in the West, to Tashhent in the South, and Vladivostok in the East. There is a diversified group of languages and cultures among the Baptists, as well as different theological directions in expression of piety and worship. Yet all of them are united in the All Union Council of Evangelical Christians-Baptists (AUCECB) of the U.S.S.R.

Many tourists visit Moscow and the Baptist church there and get a good first impression of the Baptist movement through the singing of the choirs, the moving audible prayers of the people, the impassioned preaching of the pastors, the standing-room-only crowd. Yet many of the other congregations are not as large as the 5,000-member Moscow church which has twenty-six preachers. Many of the other churches in the provinces are smaller, and sometimes composed only of women with a woman serving as pastor (though not allowed to be ordained by the brethren!).

The Baptist movement in the U.S.S.R. came from two main sources. The northern group was influenced by Lord Radstock from Great Britain and called themselves Evangelical Christians. The southern group in the Ukraine were influenced by the German settlers

The Baptist congregation in Leningrad, U.S.S.R., is bidding farewell to foreign visitors in the traditional way by waving handkerchiefs and singing "Blest be the Tie that Binds."

The communion service during the 42nd Congress of the All Union Council of Evangelical Christians-Baptists, Moscow, U.S.S.R., in 1979. Note the loaves of bread and chalices of wine.

and called themselves Baptists. They united during World War II along with the Mennonites, who are mainly German-speaking, and a group of Pentecostalists. Thus the Baptist group in the U.S.S.R.--or more correctly speaking, the AUCECB--is really the Protestant Ecumenical Council of the country. Except for the Lutherans in the Baltic states and elsewhere, most Protestants are united under the Baptists.

It is not always easy to keep such a diversified group together! Thus in 1960 a group broke away calling themselves the "initiative group." Many in the West refer to them as "dissident Baptists" or "underground Baptists." The leader of this group was Georgi Vins who is now living in the U.S.A. The break-away group poses not merely a political question or lack of religious freedom as those in the West would make it out to be. They represent a theological controversy within the U.S.S.R. among all Baptists. Must one suffer in order to be a true Christian? Can Baptists greet the patriarch as a brother in Christ? Can Baptists belong to the World Council of Churches? Should churches register with the government in order to be allowed to open? There are differences of opinions on these questions in the West.

One further concern that confronts Baptists in Europe is that of the unity of the church. Baptists in the U.S.S.R. feel that it is basic to their witness that there be only one Baptist union (convention) in the country. Independent Baptist churches, as are prevalent in the U.S.A., destroy an effective witness and lead to churches being built around a charismatic leader who often draws attention to his own leadership ability. The electronic church in the U.S.A. is a good example of this. The controversy in the U.S.S.R. is not exactly the same, but there are overtones which are similar. The independent movement among Baptists did not spread very much. At most there are probably 20,000 "initiative group" Baptists, but most of them came back into the AUCEBC in the 1970s.

Baptists in the U.S.S.R. are witnessing and rejoicing just like all Baptists around the world. More than 10,000 are baptized every year. There is a sense of revival in many of their churches, particularly in the Ukraine. A young people's choir and youth are to be found in all the churches.

The variety in the various Baptist movements in the country can be seen in Tallin, Estonia, where the Baptists meet in a large cathedral, the symbol of Tallin. This Lutheran cathedral was given to the Baptists after World War II when the Germans left. Now it is beautifully painted, the members having collected 11,000 rubles ($15,000) one Sunday. The church is packed at its three worship services on Sunday. The 2,000-member congregation is just like a Baptist cathedral should be! After the service there are groups all around who meet and have fellowship. The great organ is played by an organist who makes Bach sound beautiful. Often a symphony orchestra plays, and the 200-voice choir is outstanding. Many of the people are professionals who are involved in the local symphony! The Baptist cathedral, although large, is like the small Baptist churches in the Ukraine in that it beckons men and women to be followers of Christ.

In December, 1979, the AUCEBC met in Moscow. It was a joy to see their democratic deliberations and plans for the 1980s. There was a sense of unity and expectation. Pastors requested the leaders to work for more Bibles and permission to build more church buildings. The youth wanted to be heard, and the women said they needed to be better represented. The Baptists of the U.S.S.R. are a vitally concerned church about witnessing in all spheres of life--at times more restricted than in the West, yet perhaps more alive in the Spirit!

(YUGOSLAVIA)

When we think of Eastern Europe we do not often include Yugoslavia in this group. Yet culturally, politically, and geographically it belongs to the Eastern European more than the Western European nations. Its Tito-form of Marxism has given more freedoms than in other countries. Anyone can get a passport to leave the country if he/she chooses, and the money earned abroad is transferable on an open market. Yet the government is Marxist and the educational system is one of secular atheism.

The 3,517 Baptists in Yugoslavia are comprised of various cultural and language groups. The northern group of Croatians come mainly from Catholic backgrounds, and the southern groups of Serbians come more from an Orthodox background. There is fierce rivalry between the various cultural groups. In addition to these large groups, there are Slovenians, Hungarians, some Albanians and Romanians. Each of the Baptist groups has its own customs. When I went to one group of Slovenian Baptists, I was told not to wear a necktie, while at the next service which was Hungarian they all had ties on! One group, influenced by the Darbyites, is against an ordained clergy. Another group very strongly supports the seminary in Novi Sad.

The President of Yugoslavian Baptists, Dr. Horak, has an extensive radio ministry broadcast over Trans World Radio. He tries to unite all these various groups into one convention. Perhaps the hope is with the young people. As mentioned earlier, International Ministries was instrumental in providing funds to help in the purchase of a youth camp. Young people

come together every summer and witness to their
faith.

There are more than 800,000 Yugoslavians working in Europe, mostly in West German. A number of
Baptists pastors work among these expatriots trying
to meet their spiritual and physical needs.

Yugoslavian youth choir helps in the building of a youth camp.

Church members in Arad, Romania, devoted many hours of labor to build a new church after the government gave them permission.

Building Bethel Baptist Church in East Berlin.

CONCLUSION

The story of European Baptists is an ever changing one. Their beginnings were often accompanied with persecution, but their perseverance spread the Baptist faith throughout Europe in the nineteenth century. They have suffered defeats, division, and disappointment. This has been clearly presented by the writers in Europe. European Baptist problems are not unlike our own. But there is a quality of magnificence in what God has done and is doing through European Baptists. Perhaps we can profit from some of their experiences and insights.

Two major sections of material in this conclusion have been lifted from the reports of Maurice Entwistle and Denton Lotz. The philosophical and practical emphases complement each other, and both can help us to a deeper understanding of what this study can mean to us as American Baptists.

OBSERVATIONS ON CHRISTIANITY IN WESTERN EUROPE
Maurice S. Entwistle

As you have followed my brief summary of some of the salient features that Baptists share with Christians and fellow citizens in each of their countries in Western Europe, I am sure that you have begun to notice some features which are common to all of the areas. Many of them appear to be unique to the twentieth century. Certainly they bear the marks of our contemporary society, but closer examination reveals them to be old issues in a new form.

Alien Population Problems

Each one of the countries is dealing with significant alien populations whose traditions, values, and outlook vary considerably from the resident population. They have come for refuge to escape the turmoil associated with the departure of foreign administrations from former colonies. Frequently they have partially assimilated or admired the cultures of the host country, and they desire to identify with it. Sometimes they merely want to escape oppression or retribution in their homeland. They are immigrants. Others are migrants who strongly identify with their own culture and frequently resent the conflicting values and customs of the host country. But they have been attracted by apparent economic advantage. They only expect to remain in the country temporarily and then plan to return home.

All kinds of needs and pressures tend to push both immigrants and migrants to establish minority communities within the larger community. Although these subcultural groupings may only range from 2 to 4 percent of the overall national population, they are frequently dominant in many urban areas. All kinds of problems are created for families along the interface of this cultural clash. Families are torn apart; children grow up with deviant norms that hinder any kind of accommodation. Poverty and dire needs arise out of discrimination or ignorance. People are pushed beyond the breaking point of their capacities. Prejudice, hatred, and violence find fertile ground for their nourishment.

The needs of these peoples cry out for ministry and resolution. But these aliens tend to see the

Christian church either as the embodiment of super-human perfection and quickly become disillusioned or else they perceive Christianity as a religion which would deprive them of their own religious heritage. There is no easy way to express Christian love under these circumstances. But churches in all the industrial areas of Europe realize that Christ's neighbor is waiting for them in these communities. And in some cases, Christians are realizing that they now have a unique opportunity to meet these new residents as equals without the legal barriers found in their countries of origin.

The problem related to accommodation of alien cultures, however, is not new to Europe. Every one of these countries has had to deal with waves of migration in the past. The clash of cultures resulted in a struggle for dominance in some areas (between Celts and Saxons), in accommodation in others (Gauls and Romans), and in cleavage between others (Irish and British). No doubt similar tendencies will reoccur today. But is the church to stand aside or get involved? If it does, how?

A second observation grows out of the oil crisis and world recession which began in the mid-seventies. For the third time in this century, European nations have become aware that there seems to be a limit on the number of problems they can expect to resolve at any given time.

Confidence in Humanism Shaken

Humanism, beginning perhaps as far back as the Renaissance in the fourteenth century, was imbued with the thought that all man needed to do to solve all his problems was to harness his resources. Ignorance was his basic problem and his only limitation.

Its most extreme form is found in the European

heritage which led to the building of the American nation: When problems became too great, they pushed back the frontiers. But the day came when they had to reconcile themselves to the limits imposed by the Pacific Ocean. Whether the current situation is permanent or not, Europe seems to believe that in its role as a member of the world community it may have arrived at the limits of its own "Pacific Shores."

The mood is not one of pessimism. But there is a definite nostalgia for that recent time when social planning would solve all their problems. Suddenly, national budgets are creaking with strain as the productive resources of society are taxed to their limit to meet the social needs of the population for work, public health, and support for the deprived in their own society and elsewhere. In the unexpected confrontation with choices which condemn one to accept problems whose solution is known but for which resources are inadequate, churches are no more immune to throwing temper tantrums over denied aspirations than other pressure groups in society. And there is a real danger that contemporary man may sacrifice his freedom for a totalitarian promise to restore the "garden of Eden." People are suddenly aware that we live in considerable danger.

Our danger is not just from external threats, real as they may be. We have become aware that we are exceedingly finite and, by the wrong choices, may ourselves bring this elaborate social network which we have so slowly built up over the centuries crashing down on our heads. As everyone scrambles for the "goodies" that seem inadequate to meet everyone's needs, sensible people are suddenly crying out that our collective greediness may bring us all to unwitting destruction.

We may not be able to prevent such fatal foolishness. But the biblical injunction in the garden was that man could enjoy it as long as he was willing to impose a limit on his appetite. Sane men, both in the church and out, are saying to us that the time has come for us to set priorities and accept the pain that comes from realizing some needs must go unmet.

As countries wrestle for markets with rising Third World economies, as industrial nations pay ever higher prices for increasingly scarce materials, as Common Market fishermen struggle with the fact that they cannot all fish the same European fishbeds indefinitely, as medical research realizes that the same funds cannot be spent twice on both cancer and malaria, as schools realize they cannot provide education to cover every facet of life from the cradle to the grave, as government officials realize that there is not enough income to pay for all the desired services, and perhaps before the "goose that laid the golden egg" is starved by greed, it may be that "humanist" man will repent and accept his finitude. And if he does, who provides the criteria to select his priorities?

Still European churches tend to believe that we must not only encourage men to be good stewards of the talents the King has given us to use until his return, but we must also be ready to spend on our neighbor without hope of return. Here is tension without a ready-made answer. Do you suppose God really expects his people to search for a balance? Has he really left his creatures with the responsibility and the burden of making errors for which the innocent will suffer?

Some churches have made it a point to get involved in this discussion. Frequently, it seems they are reduced to being an advocate only for those who have no voice in society: The isolated elderly,

215

criminals quarantined in abominable prisons, the
stateless person—and so it goes until both Christian and non-Christian wonder if active, healthy,
working people count too. They do.

But what about the new doctor in Holland who
finds it almost impossible to gain a living from private practice and finds no clinic post? What about
the young person in northern Ireland who hasn't worked
since leaving school several years ago and has never
seen his father work either? What about the children
who die of malaria and kwashiorkor in some far-off
land? Do Christians have a duty to seek a hearing
for them? And do Christians also share a responsibility for reassessing the ethics of killing taxes
and bureaucratic indolence?

Churches, thank God, have lost their divine right
to imperialistic control over the minds of men. So
perhaps Christians could be more humble about their
claims to know what society's priorities ought to be.
Perhaps men and women in the church of Christ should
accept to make their voice "as one who cries in the
wilderness" and just let it be heard in the midst of
all the others. If we ask "humanist" man to recognize
his finitude, it may be we can join the human race
too and also accept our God-given finitude. But once
we have, we can be free. We can shout then, knowing
our shout is no more awe-inspiring than that of any
other mortal. We can then afford to reason quietly,
and perhaps we might even accept the defeat of our
list of priorities knowing that, strange as it may
be, even that could be within the providence of God.
When we move into Christian finitude, we are brought
face-to-face with another issue of our time.

Changing Church-State Relationships

The churches of Europe have lost the "right hand
of power" for the most part. In some cases their

privileged position shared the fate of chieftains-become-kings who were toppled from their thrones. But in many areas they still retain their feudal rights over territories that have long since ceased to bow to feudal lords. And as we have seen there have even been times when the Christian church maintained its dominion by an unholy alliance with the state. The residue of centuries of work is often found here in the claims of almost total allegiance they hold on whole peoples. Whether the symbol at the spire peak be a rooster, a plain cross, or even crosses decorated with a globe, crooked bars, a halo, or a crown, there has been little desire in the past to share their heavenly space with those who aspired after any other expression of Christian faith.

Christian churches in this part of Europe still maintain their differences. Not all want to meet each other, and it may be that some of those who do have mixed emotions. But Christians in Europe today are conversing in a way that their fathers might not have thought possible, not to say anything about its desirability. There is little likelihood that we shall resolve all our differences in the foreseeable future. But let us thank God for those places where joint prayer has replaced reciprocal anathemas.

We need to pray. Many have called this area "post-Christian" Europe. They point with alarm, or horror, or disdain at the low numbers of people who actually attend worship services. And it is true. But before we wash our hands of the Christian church in Europe, let us just take a moment to look at this situation a bit more closely. It has been a long, hard road to get this far--almost two thousand years long, in fact.

In early European tribal society religion was perceived as a supernatural social power which protected their people and assured them of victory.

Their rulers were intimately associated with this power. Their reign was both dependent on religious practices and was understood as an expression of spiritual power. Individuals no more thought of abandoning tribal or clan religious practices than they would consider betraying their clan leader or tribal chief. The introduction of competitive religious practices from another area was feared as a source of possible calamity or as a vehicle for rival power and social upheaval. It is no wonder then that early Christianity often made its most significant impact in areas where tribal leaders would accept Christianity.

This was, as much as our modern mindset may find the idea difficult to conceive, perhaps the only door into such barbarian cultures. The very fact that it took upwards of seven centuries for Christianity to make even nominal inroads into this area should be an indication of the difficulties involved. It was only natural, under these circumstances, that Christianity was expected to perform the same social functions for the regions it took over as had the previous religious practices--only better!

In other words, not only did Christianity have expectations about those who would accept Christ, even so, and in some respects even more importantly, society had expectations of Christianity as a religion. Remember that these presuppositions had probably been a tacit assumption of primitive peoples for thousands of years. Such cultural baggage is not shed just because one passes through the waters of baptism.

So Christianity in Western Europe, as elsewhere, automatically became a carrier of culture with, as the expression goes, "all rights and privileges thereunto belonging." Christianity was, so to speak, a civic function for these peoples.

These civic presuppositions about the religious function of Christianity—as a repository for the spiritual power of society, as a privileged relationship for the rulers and a sanction for their authority, as the channel by which kith and kin gave unquestioning obedience to the elders who had consulted religious authorities and had made their decision—all these and more were inherited by the new faith when it entered these alien cultures and replaced tribal religions.

It took centuries for the struggle which was implicit in the Christian faith to work itself through to conscious cultural expression. And if these factors weren't enough, it was further complicated by other ones.

As different subcultures vied for power on the Continent, Christianity often served as the major carrier of cultural values that assured a people of their identity because of its role in enshrining their positive traditions, in enhancing their language and literature, and in providing an alternative social structure to help them resist acculturation. This was behind the reason that Celtic and Saxon forms of Christianity found such great difficulty in resolving their differences, and this can still be found behind the opposition between Irish and English forms of Christianity.

The Reformation was only one of many forms of dissent that arose to promote a transition from a collective approach to authority to a sense of personal responsibility for decision making. That European man was not yet ready to adopt this teaching, which Hebrew prophets had imparted centuries earlier (Ezekiel 33:12-20), is proved by the fact that it only flourished where local rulers encouraged it to enhance their own power. Dissent within each prince's territory was as severely punished as the reigning Haps-

burgs would have liked to have imposed on their subject princes, had they been able. Society didn't
really question the principle of a ruler's right to
decide for his people. It was still only a question
of the relative power rulers had or could impose.
The right of dissent or a loyal opposition had yet
to evolve.

One of the fundamental contributions of our age,
let us say with the rise of the Free Churches and
the struggle for religious liberty, was social recognition that the exercise of a private conscience was
not necessarily a denial of social authority nor a
threat to it. This was a major contribution derived
from the stubborn witness of Mennonite, Baptist,
Methodist, and other Free Churches which placed an
emphasis, at least in the initial phase of their ap-
pearance, on the need for a personal decision about
Christ regardless of one's social affiliation.

More recently Christianity has served as a vehicle for the affirmation of a people while they
awaited more adequate social rights within a society.
Such was the role of the Roman Catholic Church for
Italian Americans and the Baptist Church for American Blacks. Note that this is a different phenomenon
from that which has served in the past to maintain
identity through social opposition, as in the Presby-
terian Church's role in limiting English influence
in Scotland or the Roman Catholic Church's role in
Ireland for the same purposes. In the latter case,
it has led to division. In the case of American
Italians and Blacks, it has led in the former to
full integration in a pluralistic society, and in
time it may well do so for the latter.

In all these cases we find that the Christian
church has served as a vital carrier of perceived
and unperceived cultural values, which may be important but are only secondary to its primary mission

of declaring the Good News.

This cultural burden has been a heavy load for the Christian church down through the ages. Despite many failures, the Christian church has, nevertheless, discharged its task well, and many of the values found in the gospel and in man's heritage are now consciously incorporated into the value structures of society. In modern times we have seen society assuming for itself those values and roles which the Christian church has rightly taught belong to social institutions.

Sometimes this process has been premature. This has been particularly so when the church had not yet learned to depend upon freely accorded consent and still used absolute power. On such occasions the stripping of power from the church merely meant that the monolithic approach to cultural norms was appropriated by the state, i.e., as in Franco's Spain or Marxist Russia.

But in this part of Europe the process seems to be evolving satisfactorily. The Christian church merely appears to have lost ground. In point of fact the church is now able to identify more easily those to whom it should address the question it carries to every generation: "Have you met Jesus Christ, and will you accept him as Lord and Savior?" "Post-Christian" Europe is probably no more an appropriate term to describe the current situation than "Christian" Europe was to describe the previous state.

The Baptist Contribution

Baptist churches here in Europe have emphasized the right of each person to make his own choice before God and to enter or refuse to enter the church on the basis of personal choice. Our churches are not unique in calling attention to man's decision-making capacity nor to his need to make a decision about this question. Confirmation, in many other churches, is an attempt to meet this need. But Baptists have exercised a catalytic function in calling on society and the church to pay more than lip service to religious liberty. Baptists paid a high price for announcing this principle when it was unpopular to do so. But they have been heard, and this truth has been given general recognition in society today.

So our distinctives may now be less distinctive in this part of Europe than they once were. And some of the truths we hold together in the Christian church may be more distinctive to today's society than they might have appeared to be in the past. So the work of Christ will continue to fulfill the task which God has placed before them here and everywhere until he comes.

WHAT CAN WE LEARN FROM EASTERN EUROPEAN BAPTISTS?
Denton Lotz

In 1979 the European Baptists held their once-every-five-year Congress in Brighton, England. The motto was "Weak, yet so strong." European Baptists are weak compared to the more than 30 million Baptists of all persuasions in the U.S.A. The more than a million European Baptists compose a minority, and in some countries are treated as ignorant sectarians or foolish religionists. Yet in their weakness the Baptists in Eastern Europe have come to understand more what the Apostle Paul meant when he said, "When I am weak, then I am strong (2 Corinthians 12:10)."

We were in Moscow in 1975 when the U.S. and the U.S.S.R. were celebrating the "victory over fascism," the 30th anniversary of the defeat of Nazi Germany. Millions were in the streets, and the display of military equipment showed the great power of the armies of this world. That Sunday at the Baptist church about 2,000 were gathered. When I greeted them with the Easter greeting "Christos Voskres" ("Christ is Risen"), all stood up and shouted, "He is risen indeed!" How odd it must seem to the world. The millions with their military power and these poor thousands saying "Christ crucified--risen." He is the power of God. This is the paradox of faith. It is the paradox of the Baptist witness in Eastern Europe. Weak in number, weak in ability to influence culture, weak in educational opportunities, yet strong in the power that only Christ can give, strong in the hope of his coming, strong to love all--capitalist or communist, weak or strong, rich or poor.

There is much that Baptists in the U.S.A. can learn from their brothers and sisters in Eastern Europe. In this new era of mission it is not only that we are a "sending" church, but we must also become a "receiving" church. We need to learn from each other.

Witnessing to One's Faith

To be a Christian means to witness to one's faith. It is a contagious faith; once having experienced it, one wants to share the Good News with all. This can be done by word and deed. However, often we are embarrassed to speak about our faith. This fear may come from lack of confidence or insecurity, or in some cases lack of knowledge about one's faith. Our churches need to encourage one another by a form of "team witnessing" where two or three go out together to visit and witness. But, it need not be that formal. At work, at school, at play--these are no clichés--but really that is the place where the lay person can really be an effective witness! An old lady in Moscow came to her pastor last December and was very upset. The pastor inquired what was wrong. She said that she had promised the Lord to bring twelve new souls to Christ in the year. And it was now December and she had brought only seven new people. Imagine if every Baptist in the U.S.A. would bring only one!

Holiness

"Puritanism" is a term which has been disregarded today because it has become associated with a legalistic understanding of the faith which tries to force certain ways of behavior on others. It is often a Christian faith that has lost its fire and is often bound up with rules and "do's and don't's." However, originally Puritanism was concerned about holiness-- a life lived in an exemplary way showing the purifying power of the Holy Spirit. Holiness need not be a drab or arrogant way of life. It can be a humble witness to a changed life. I dare say that the holy life of the believers in Eastern Europe is one of the most important means of evangelism.

Biblical Preaching

Around the world all Christians would say that the Bible is the source and norm of their faith. Yet, much of our preaching is not biblical preaching. It is a preaching which uses biblical texts as an afterthought to a main thought A rediscovery of biblical preaching would revolutionize not only our preaching but our church life. Professor Heremias from Germany once told me after a discussion of the lack of seriousness in biblical study among students, "But my hope is that the power of God is in the Bible." Every renewal and reformation in the church has come from a rediscovery of the Bible, not in some head-in-the-sand-type of preaching but a fresh openness to the Holy Spirit.

Patience

I met a man from Lithuania who had waited forty years to visit friends in the West. Many churches wait ten or more years for permission to build. There is a patience, a holy patience, that our friends in Eastern Europe have that we need. Sometimes we need to stop all our activity and to listen to the Psalmist, "My soul waits for the Lord, more than the watchman waits for the morning." Patience would help us to redirect our goals towards God's will in our lives.

Simple Lifestyle

Many refugees to the U.S.A. are horrified to visit our stores and to see the surplus of luxury foods, luxury toys, consumer goods, etc., when they know that back home their families are trying just to make it through another week. Part of a holy life and a dedicated life would express itself, I think, in a simpler lifestyle. Many books on world hunger are encouraging us to think in this direction. The reality of life in Eastern Europe also forces us to ponder the question anew.

Ways in Which We Can Help

Americans are a wonderfully pragmatic people. I have noticed this again since coming back after many years abroad. We want to do something, to get the job done--right away! The European is often more patient and philosophical about situations. "Wait a little, and let's see how the situation develops." "We've tried it before many years ago and it won't work." "The government will never allow it." These are common attitudes we have all heard before even in our own country.

What can we do? We can do quite a lot. In

fact, the American Baptists since 1945 have done very much for Baptists in Europe and especially in Eastern Europe. During the post World War II period, millions of dollars have been sent for various church-related programs in Europe, including buildings, scholarships, medicines, books, etc.

We Can Pray

Prayer unites us around the world with what the Holy Spirit is doing. It awakens our interest in specific places, and it is God's voice speaking to us to act and to be alert to our duties. Prayer is not a passive exercise to put us asleep to the harsh realities of life. On the contrary, the prayer of the community is the utterance of the Spirit, pushing us always forward into God's new work of love and redemption. He who prays for Eastern Europe will not sit back and think his deed is done. It will lead him further.

We Can Become Informed

Prayer should lead us to be better informed about that for which we are praying. There is much misinformation about Eastern Europe. Much of the material that is read in the U.S.A. goes back to the Stalinist period when there was very harsh persecution and imprisonment of believers. Stories of Bible smuggling often go back to this cold war period. In some written material I have seen, there are no dates when incidents are related about Bibles, etc. To be better informed, one should read denominational material on the progress of the church. Also, the regional reports, such as come from the European Baptist Federation and the Baptist World Alliance, provide a wealth of information on what the churches are doing in Eastern and Western Europe.

We Can Change Our Minds

It was a surprise for me the first time I visited the U.S.S.R. to see the many people in church. I was not prepared for this when I first visited the church in Leningrad in 1959. My mind was filled with images of "propaganda," "show," etc. But then when I prayed with them, heard them sing, and saw their deep expression of faith and observed as they shared their testimony and witnessed to me of their faith and observed as they shared their testimony and witnessed to me of their faith in Christ, I had to change my mind. I had to admit that I had prejudices which were unfair. To be sure, it was a communist system. Of course, atheism was taught in the schools. Yes, there were restrictions upon the church. BUT, in spite of it all the church was flourishing. It was alive, and many men and women were being baptized and coming to faith in Christ. These were not "show worship services." These were real experiences of the Holy Spirit breaking through the various barriers that all mankind is inclined to set up, be they in New York, in Moscow, or Peking!

We Can Visit Churches Abroad

I am surprised at the number of American Baptists who often visit Europe and see the big cathedrals but never take an opportunity to visit the little Baptist church on the side street. True, these Baptist churches do not represent the great cultural history of Europe, but they do represent our Baptist faith and practice, our history of suffering and witness. Every large city in Europe has a Baptist church. Your hotel can probably give you the name and location of local Baptist churches, whether in Moscow or Budapest. International Ministries' office in Valley Forge may also provide a list of Baptist churches in the various capitals.

We Can Provide Financial Support

If you want to help Baptists, the best way I feel is through the Baptist groups in the countries. Through International Ministries and the Baptist World Alliance we have daily contact with the leaders and churches. We know what projects are urgently in progress and where funds are needed. This is true whether it is for churches in Hungary, or an old people's home in Poland, or scholarship money for students to SITE, or money for a car, or medical aid for a cripple, or books, or Bibles. Give through Baptist channels, and you can be sure that you are reaching the needs of your brothers and sisters! An old man in Budapest came up to me and said, "I don't know you but I love you." Your brothers and sisters throughout Eastern Europe who have been the beneficiaries of your gifts would want me to thank you and say, "With all our hearts we love you in Jesus Christ."

A children's choir in Budapest, Hungary.

APPENDIX I

MINUTES OF A MEETING CALLED TO FORM THE
EUROPEAN BAPTIST FEDERATION
held at 48 Rue de Lille, Paris (7)
on Friday and Saturday, 20th and
21st of October, 1950

Friday, October 20

1. Those Attending

The following representatives of Baptist unions
were present:

Rev. Carl Alder	Switzerland
Rev. Henry Cook, M.A.	Great Britain & Ireland
Rev. Alfred K. Dahl	Norway
Rev. A. A. Hardenberg	Netherlands
Rev. Hans Luckey, Ph.D.	Germany
Rev. Bredahl Petersen, Ph.D.	Denmark
Rev. Manfredi Ronchi	Italy
Rev. Victor Sedaca	Spain
Rev. Ruben Swedberg	Sweden
Rev. Henri Vincent	France
Rev. W. O. Lewis, Ph.D.	Baptist World Alliance

In addition the following were also present and
were invited to take part in the meeting:

Rev. H. V. Larcombe, B.A., B.D., representing
the Continental Committee of the Baptist
Union of Great Britain and Ireland.
Rev. Vincenzo Veneziano from Italy.
Rev. W. T. Cowlan, representing the Young

People's Department of the Baptist Union of
Great Britain and Ireland.
Rev. Hans C. Barkan, representing the Bap-
tist Boy Scouts of Denmark.

Greetings were received from Dr. Edwin A. Bell,
Dr. H. Mascher, Rev. M. Kolomainen, Rev. A. Sund-
quist, Rev. A. Mauricio, and Dr. J. Nordenhaug.

Hans Luckey and Henry Cook opened the meeting
with prayer.

2. Temporary Chairman

It was unanimously agreed that W. O. Lewis
should serve in this capacity.

3. Minute Secretary

It was unanimously agreed that W. T. Cowlan
should be asked to keep the minutes.

4. History of the Movement

W. O. Lewis welcomed all present and outlined
briefly the steps which had led to a closer fellowship of European Baptists. He stated that
he had attended the first All-European Baptist
Conference in Berlin in 1908, when it was hoped
there would be a similar conference between the
world congresses of the Alliance.

The next European Baptist conference was held
in Stockholm in 1913.

After the first World War it was impossible to
hold a European conference, but instead regional
conferences were held. The first was in connection with a visit of President E. Y. Mullins
in 1926. Again in 1930, conferences were held

in connection with a Presidential visit of Dr. John MacNeill. A third series was held on the occasion of a visit of President George W. Truett in 1937.

At a Conference called by the Alliance in London in 1948, a Committee of Seven was appointed to launch a scheme for the closer integration of European Baptists. This Committee met in Rüschlikon, Zürich, on the 8th of October, 1949, and drew up a constitution and a plan for a European Baptist Federation. This plan had been submitted to as many of the Baptist unions of Europe as could be reached. General approval of the plan had been expressed by Great Britain, Denmark, Norway, Sweden, Germany, Holland, France, Switzerland, and Italy.

The provisional constitution drafted in Rüschlikon, Zürich, October 8, 1949, was laid before the meeting, and after certain changes had been made, the constitution was adopted.

Dr. Lewis declared that the European Baptist Federation was duly formed and called for the election of officers.

5. Election of Officers

Messrs. Cowlan and Barkan were asked to pass out and collect the ballot papers. The following were declared elected:

> President: Dr. Bredahl Petersen
> Vice-President: Henry Cook
> Secretary-Treasurer pro tem: W. L. Lewis

Immediately after the election, Dr. Lewis called upon Dr. Petersen to take the chair.

231

6. President's Remarks

Dr. Petersen thanked all for the confidence the brethren had reposed in him. He expressed appreciation of the work of Dr. Lewis in bringing about such a federation. He also hoped this organization would help to make all European Baptists continentally-minded.

7. Election of Executive Committee

In addition to the elected officers who serve ex officio, the following were elected as members of the Executive Committee of the Council of the Federation:

Henri Vincent, A. A. Hardenberg, Hans Luckey, and Manfredi Ronchi.

8. Council Meeting

It was agreed that the next meeting of the Council should be held in Hamburg, August 2-6, 1951. It was agreed that the delegates should assemble by midday on Thursday and that their services be utilized by the Baptist churches in Hamburg and vicinity during the weekend.

9. European Conference

It was agreed that the first All-European Conference of the Federation should be held in Copenhagen July 29 to August 3, 1952.

It was agreed that the Conference should be preceded by a full meeting of the Council on Tuesday morning the 29th of July, and the Conference should begin at 2:00 p.m. the same day. It was suggested that the woman and the young people should be responsible for the meetings on Wednes-

day and Saturday respectively, and that there
be sectional meetings for ministers and laymen.

10. Plans for 1950/51

A general discussion followed concerning plans
for the ensuing two years.

The President suggested that various commissions
should be set up, and that the possibility of
opening up work in certain places where there is
no Baptist church should be explored.

On behalf of the Baptist young people of Europe,
W. T. Cowlan thanked the President for the privilege of taking part in the meeting. He reported
that at a recent meeting of Baptist youth leaders
in Holland, the hope was expressed that the
European Baptist Federation would sponsor youth
camps, and they were interested in establishing
a Baptist church in Strasbourg. They also hoped
a news bulletin would be published.

On behalf of the Continental Committee of the
Baptist Union of Great Britain and Ireland, H. V.
Larcombe said his Committee welcomed the setting
up of this Federation. It should serve as a
clearing house of ideas for European Baptists.
His Committee would like guidance concerning
priorities in Europe. He thought perhaps all
the Baptists of Europe should help rebuild the
Böhmkenstrasse church in Hamburg as a memorial
to Oncken. He wondered about the needs in Finland. He announced that the Scripture Gift Mission was willing to supply portions of Scripture
for distribution on the Continent.

After considerable discussion, it was agreed
that Dr. Lewis should consult with Dr. Luckey
concerning the building of the Oncken Memorial

Church in Hamburg, and that they should report to the Council later.

11. News Bulletin

It was unanimously agreed that the Federation should issue a newssheet. It was also agreed that Henry Cook should be appointed to gather news and send out such a newsletter.

There being no further business, the meeting adjourned.

In the evening the Avenue du Maine Church gave a reception to the visitors in its chapel.

Saturday, October 21

The delegates assembled again for business in the Rue de Lille building on Saturday morning. The Scripture was read by Dr. Bredahl Petersen and prayer was offered by M. Ronchi.

12. Various Projects

Dr. Petersen led in a discussion of various projects which the Federation might undertake. Before beginning the consideration of common tasks in the future, he expressed the appreciation of all for the contribution being made to Baptist work in Europe by the Seminary in Rüschlikon, Zürich. He hoped there would always be close and friendly relations between this institution and the European Baptist Federation.

It was agreed that the following objects should have priority for the next few years:
(a) The building of an Oncken Memorial Church in Hamburg as an expression of European Baptist unity.

234

(b) In view of the importance of Strasbourg as headquarters of the Council of Europe, a serious effort should be made to establish a Baptist church in that city. It was felt that first of all a worker with a knowledge of French and German should be found and put to work on this field. The French and Swiss Baptists should take the lead in finding such a man, and the Baptists of Europe and America should be asked to provide funds for his support for the first few years.

(c) In view of opportunities now existing in Spain, it was felt that the Baptists in Hispanic America should be urged to enter these open doors.

(d) Having heard from A. K. Dahl the account of the progress in securing a site for a theological school in Oslo, and having learned that the American Baptist Foreign Mission Society is willing to provide dollar for dollar for this school up to $50,000, it was agreed that the Baptists of Europe should be urged to make contributions to help Norwegian Baptists to complete this project.

(e) After discussion of the needs of the Finnish-speaking Baptists in Finland, it was agreed to refer this matter for advice to the Scandinavian Baptist Council. It was agreed that a Finnish hymnbook is needed.

13. Women and Young People

It was agreed to invite the European Baptist Women's organization and the Baptist young people of Europe to be represented in the meeting of the Council to be held in Hamburg in August, 1951. Other Baptist unions not represented at this meeting are to be informed of the organization of the European Baptist Federation and are urged to join.

14. Evangelism

Discussion ensued on evangelism and the part the
Federation could most usefully play in its furtherance. Dr. Luckey said that in his opinion
such work should be carried out by the nationals
in the various countries, and must always be
related to the local churches where converts
would receive baptism and find a spiritual home.
He urged the need of prayer by all for all.

15. Day of Prayer

It was agreed that the last Sunday in October
should be observed in all the unions as a Day
of Prayer for Europe, this being the Sunday
nearest to the day the European Baptist Federation was founded. The President would suggest
subjects for prayer on that day. All were urged
to pray earnestly for the Baptists in Eastern
Europe.

16. Foreign Missions

Attention was called to the fact that the Baptists in certain countries in Europe have no
missin work in non-Christian lands. Those de-
siring to undertake such work were advised to
communicate with the Secretary who would endeavor to guide them in the fulfillment of their
desires.

17. The Press

It was agreed to ask Henri Vincent to notify the
press agencies of the information of this Federation.

18. <u>Thanks</u>

The President was asked to express at the public
meeting to follow in the evening the thanks of
all the delegates present, to the Baptists of
Paris for the excellent arrangements for receiving the visitors, and for the generous hospital-
ity in caring for them.

Business being finished, the Council adjourned with
prayer at noon.

On Saturday evening there was a well-attended public
meeting in the Rue de Lille building at which representatives of various countries spoke.

On Sunday morning following, H. V. Larcombe preached
to the French congregation meetings in the Avenue du
Maine church, and W. O. Lewis preached to the French
congregation in Rue de Lille church. On Sunday after-
noon W. O. Lewis preached to a Romanian congregation
in Rue de Lille. At night in the same building there
was an Anglo-French service at which Henry Cook
preached.

APPENDIX II

CONSTITUTION OF THE EUROPEAN BAPTIST FEDERATION
Adopted in Paris the 20th October, 1950

PREAMBLE

The suggestion to form a European Baptist Committee on Cooperation arose out of the work of the Baptist World Alliance and directly from recommendations made during meetings held under its auspices in London in August, 1948.

I. NAME

European Baptist Federation

II. PURPOSE

The purpose of the Federation is:

(1) to promote fellowship among Baptists in Europe,
(2) to stimulate and coordinate evangelism in Europe,
(3) to provide a board of consultation and planning for Baptist mission work in Europe,
(4) to stimulate and coordinate where desirable the foreign missionary work of European Baptists who have no field of their own,
(5) to promote such Baptist relief work as may be needed in Europe.

III. MEMBERSHIP

The members of the European Baptist Federation shall be those European unions of Baptist churches which are members of the Baptist World Alliance.

IV. OFFICERS

The officers of the European Baptist Federation shall
be a President, a Vice-President, a Secretary, and a
Treasurer, elected by and from the General Council.
The election shall ordinarily take place in connection with the All-European Baptist Conference. The
officers shall serve for two years or until their
successors are elected.

V. GENERAL COUNCIL AND EXECUTIVE

The Federation shall work through (a) a General Council, (b) an Executive Committee.

(a) The General Council shall consist of:
--one representative from each Baptist union in
    Europe belonging to the Baptist World Alliance
    chosen by the union or its committees,
--one representative from each Baptist mission-
    ary society or board or committee working regu-
    larly in Europe,
--the Associate General Secretary of the Baptist
    World Alliance,
--the president and secretary of the European
    Baptist Women's Union and the European Baptist
    Youth organization as well as similar officers
    of such auxiliary organizations as the General
    Council shall from time to time approve,
--the Executive Committee of the Baptist World
    Alliance shall be asked to nominate not more
    than five of its European members to serve on
    the General Council of the European Baptist
    Federation.

(b) The Executive Committee shall consist of seven
members which shall include the officers. It
shall have authority to carry on the work of the
Federation between the meetings of the General
Council.

VI. WAYS AND MEANS

The Federation shall seek to achieve its purposes by such means as the following:

(1) General conferences of all the Baptist unions of Europe,
(2) Regional conferences,
(3) International training courses and fellowship meetings,
(4) The exchange of ministers, evangelists, theological teachers, students, and other leaders in various church activities.

VII. ALTERATION OF THE CONSTITUTION

This Constitution can be altered only at a meeting of the General Council, called after the proposed alteration has been referred to the member unions, and then only by a two-thirds majority of union representatives present and voting.

APPENDIX III

EUROPEAN BAPTIST FEDERATION
SECRETARY/TREASURERS

1950-1955	W. O. Lewis	U.S.A.
1955-1960	Henry Cook	England
1960-1965	Erik Rudén	Sweden
1965-1975	Ronald Goulding	England
1975-1980	Gerhard Claas	Germany
1980-	Knud Wümpelmann	Denmark